AFRIKAKORPS

SELF PORTRAIT

DAL McGUIRK

AFRIKAKORPS

SELF PORTRAIT

Airlife
England

DEDICATION

This book is dedicated to the memory of Friedrich Kägebein,
a twenty-year-old grenadier in the 7th Company Panzergrenadier Regiment
104, killed at El Alamein in October 1942, as representing all the men and
women on both sides who died in North Africa during World War II.

Copyright © Dal McGuirk 1992

First published in the UK in 1992
by Airlife Publishing Ltd.

British Library Cataloguing in Publication Data
A catalogue record of this book
is available from the British Library.

ISBN 185310 327 6

Printed by Livesey Ltd., Shrewsbury, England.

Airlife Publishing Ltd.
101 Longden Road, Shrewsbury, Shropshire SY3 9EB

CONTENTS

	Acknowledgements
	Introduction
CHAPTER 1	Fatherland
CHAPTER 2	The Army in Europe, at Home and at War
CHAPTER 3	Transit: Goodbye Germany, Hello Africa
CHAPTER 4	Before and After
CHAPTER 5	Typically African
CHAPTER 6	Rommel
CHAPTER 7	Camp Scenes
CHAPTER 8	Faces
CHAPTER 9	Food and Drink
CHAPTER 10	In General
CHAPTER 11	Camouflage
CHAPTER 12	Rest and Relaxation
CHAPTER 13	In Battle — Under Fire
CHAPTER 14	Artillery
CHAPTER 15	Infantry, African Grenadiers
CHAPTER 16	Medical
CHAPTER 17	Motorcycle Battalion
CHAPTER 18	PAK and Flak
CHAPTER 19	Panzers
CHAPTER 20	Pioneers
CHAPTER 21	Reconnaissance
CHAPTER 22	Signals
CHAPTER 23	Transport and Supply
CHAPTER 24	Graves
CHAPTER 25	The Enemy
CHAPTER 26	The Italians
CHAPTER 27	The End, Tunisia 1943
CHAPTER 28	For the Record
CHAPTER 29	Ernst Zwilling

The Principle Moral Elements

They are: *the skill of the commander, the experience and courage of the troops, and their patriotic spirit.* The relative value of each cannot be universally established; it is hard enough to discuss their potential, and even more difficult to weigh them against each other. The wisest course is not to underate any of them — a temptation to which human judgment, being fickle, often succumbs. It is preferable to muster historical evidence of the unmistakable evidence of all three.

Efficiency, skill, and the tempered courage that welds the body of troops into a single mould will have their greatest scope in operations in open country.

Carl von Clausewitz, *On War*

Quotation from *On War* by Carl von Clausewitz, edited and translated by Michael Howard and Peter Paret 1976, reproduced by permission of Princeton University Press, Princeton, New Jersey.

ACKNOWLEDGEMENTS

The photos reproduced in this book came from a variety of sources, from former soldiers on both sides of the fighting in North Africa, from friends and relatives, from militaria dealers and from fellow collectors. To everyone who helped in my search for original wartime photos I owe more than I can measure. Without their interest and assistance such a book of photos as this would obviously not have been possible.

For photos obtained from old soldiers, in New Zealand I had the assistance of the members of the 21 NZ Infantry Battalion Association, especially the ever-gracious Tony Ivicevich; and in Germany I was again fortunate to have the wonderful help of Karl-Heinz Böttger, Oberst a.D., and my good friends from the Association of Former Members of the 2nd Company, Sonderverband 288 — Dr (med) Manfred Auberlen; Werner Kost, Major a.D.; Hans Müller; Willi Prell; Andreas Rein; the late Franz Seidl; Alois Stockmayer; Joachim Thümser; Fritz Wenger.

I am indebted to Dieter Hellriegel for photos connected with Rommel's *Begleitkommando* (Escort Squad) in 1941 and from Rommel's *Kampfstaffel* (Battle Squadron) in 1942 and 1943.

For all the former members of the *Afrikakorps* who have shared their memories of Africa with me, I owe a debt of gratitude I can never repay. It was you who made the photos come alive for me; you shared those glimpses I would otherwise not have seen.

I thank Helmut Weitze for leading me to the personal photo albums of the late Georg Briel, with his photos relating to (Army) Fla. Battalion 606 and PzGrenRgt 200, the units which he commanded in Africa.

Two families in particular took special interest in my work on this book, and encouraged me in my working on it with their love and friendship: Jos and Hans Schilling, and Patsy and Dick LaFayette. These two families, who share the roles of godparents to my two children, Emma and Karl, incidentally also gave me photos which are reproduced in this book.

I owe a special debt of gratitude to my good friend Charlie Hinz for his generous offer to provide photos for this book taken by the *Afrikakorps* chief official photographer, Ernst Zwilling, photos that came from Ernst Zwilling's own private collection of photos he had taken in Africa.

I had the willing help of my wife Christine, my daughter Emma, and our friend Kate Lange in the long job of matching a thousand photos with the right captions. Thanks.

And for everyone else, in alphabetical order, with warm thanks: Birgit Andreas; Russel Andrews; the late Major (ret'd) Ted Andrews; Gary Armitage; Siegfried Augustin; the late Robert Borchardt; Herbert Brandhoff; Gregory N. Carter; Alan Coates; Peter Cue; Alan Culhane; Horst Dahlke; John Damon; Jörn Dressel;

ACKNOWLEDGEMENTS CONT.

Dr Hans H. Duesel; Sepp and Joan Egger; the late Jürgen Eichler; Malcolm Fisher; Kerry Foster, Walter Fromm, Major a.D.; Robert Gilmore; Konrad Günzel; Dieter and Otti Hellriegel; Peter Hill; David Hunter; John Keener; Antoine Lebel; Bob Lyons; Paul Kenwary; Wayne McDonald; Kerry Thomas McGee; Ron Manion; Alois Marcata; John Nicholson; Detlev Niemann; Hans Neumann; David Oldham; Geoffrey P. Oldham; George A. Petersen; Heinz and Lydia Puschmann; Rüdiger Rinklef; Manfred Rommel; Adolf Rössler; Marlis Schroten; Rudolf Schulz; the late Carl Theodor Toepfer, Oberfeldvet, d.R.; Dieter Sandbeck; Paul Erich and Ingrid Schläfer; Robert Sevier; Keith Skilton; Peter Steger; Rex Trye; the late Wally von Schramm; Paul Wansbrough; Kurt Watermann; Alan Webb; Phil Wernham, Jan Wessels.

For printing the black and white photos that were copied in Auckland, a big 'thank you' goes to Ruth Rowland and Marcel de Ruiter of PCLab in Parnell, Sue Campbell of 'Black and Bright' in Ponsonby, and Barbara Ross and Harley Wilson from GM Studios in Onehunga.

Unless otherwise credited, the photos reproduced in this book are from the author's collection.

Dal McGuirk, Auckland, May 1991.

Manfred Rommel, Lord Mayor of Stuttgart and son of the Field Marshal, with the author.

INTRODUCTION

There are two very different types of photos available for anyone interested in researching the pictorial record of the German side of the war in North Africa from 1941 to 1943. First there are the collections of photos kept by many state and military libraries in the former belligerent countries, containing for the most part photos shot in Africa by German army and propaganda news photographers.

These photos were mainly, though not solely, taken to record an official view of the war in Africa, and to show it to the wartime German population through newspapers and magazines. This official pictorial view closely corresponded with the militaristic ideology promoted by the propaganda organs in wartime Germany. The army photographers were experienced professionals who had good cameras and their work showed careful framing and composition. They worked near the front in order to get the best possible action shot and many of these men were killed while using their cameras. These photographers were assigned by the *Wehrmacht* to every front in World War II where German soldiers fought, to record scenes of their day-to-day existence and the battles they fought and died in.

Looking through the negative film strips snapped by these *Wehrmacht* photographers, one sees the care they took to get the 'right' shot in just the way they wanted it from the number of slightly different views of one subject, taken from a variety of angles to get the one really effective photo. They made certain that their photos showed to the best advantage clear details of the soldiers' faces, their uniforms with medals and equipment, and their weapons. All of these things were accorded proper attention in line with the recognition given at the time to the heroic military face of the German nation at war.

In Africa, and in other theatres too, the 'battle' scenes however were not always shot during actual fighting. Some photos purporting to show 'battle' scenes were taken during what were obviously training sessions, staged somewhere away from the front but giving a realistic impression of battlefield combat. (The evidence that this is so can be seen on the strips of negative film that show posed 'battle' scenes interspersed with other views of the 'battle' being set up in front of the cameras.) In North Africa it was extremely difficult to get good clear photos while the fighting was going on. The main actors were usually on the move and could not be stage-managed to best close range effect. The open desert was too vast, the soldiers too dispersed, for the familiar scale of warfare and backdrops that had been captured on film in Europe. In any case, most desert fighting did not take place at close range. In reality the enemy were usually no more than dots on the horizon among the clouds of dust thrown up by exploding artillery shells, or totally obscured by the haze caused by the extreme daytime heat. The truest photos were those taken during lulls in the fighting, showing the faces of the soldiers themselves rather than scenes of actual desert combat.

9

When looking at the large numbers of press release photos and official military photos taken by these German armed forces photographers, housed today in various institutional archives, one gets a feeling of having seen the same photos, somewhere else and at a different time. Seen together these German photos bear a close resemblance to the photos taken by the wartime photographers on the Allied side. Instead of the lines of German and Italian prisoners one is used to seeing, here are crowds of captured British or American soldiers. Rather than seeing photos of German dead, here the bodies are Allied dead. In place of the burning Panzers, there are burning Shermans, Grants and Crusaders. Whether viewed from the German or Allied side, the face of war recorded by the teams of official photographers in North Africa looked much the same from the middle distance. Only at close range could one see the different uniforms and badges that distinguished the two sides.

The propaganda element so effective in portraying a biased view of events during the war still confuses the reliability of some wartime photos as an accurate record of what happened. German military photographers, like their Allied counterparts, sometimes snapped an artificially contrived scene to play up some aspect of official propaganda. When published, the 'truth' of such photos was much harder to challenge than the stories where dishonest words could be sniffed out. After all, the photo was like a mirror held up to the time and place, was it not? Even today it is not easy to decide which wartime photos were arranged by photographers to suit their military and political masters. One famous example of this practice, from the Allied side in North Africa, was where an APFU photographer in Tunisia grabbed 'the most evil looking Arab' he could find and snapped him wearing German helmet (with French tricolour!) and German army sweater as an example of the 'Master Race'.

Certain photographs, however, snapped by the teams of military photographers were not meant for propaganda use. They were intended as the German *Wehrmacht*'s own picture record of the campaign. To prevent these photos from being mixed up with press release photos, the army's own photos all had the distinctive stamp on the back. *Nur für den Dienstgebrauch*, 'For Service Use Only'. With the exception of exercises being photographed for use as training aids, showing the correct and approved way of doing something, these photos were very much a straight record of what happened. The captions were generally more factual and informative too. One section of these photos is included here to show just what went into the German army's own wartime photo albums as the official 'self portrait' of the *Afrikakorps*.

The second main category of photos that cover the campaign in North Africa are those taken by the ordinary German soldiers themselves, and these make up the majority of photos in this book. Unfortunately for the student of the North African war, collections of these private photos are not housed in large and centrally located storage points, all conveniently filed and catalogued. These unofficial photos are now well scattered, some still in the possession of their original owners, or with their families, while others are in the hands of their old enemies.

When I started to gather the material for this book, I had intended using a mixture of official and private photos, with rather more of the former because of the much higher 'professional' quality. The market appeal of such a book containing many striking and previously unpublished photos was obvious, especially if using only the cream of those photos obtained from state and military archives. However, I realised that the overall view given by such an assortment, using mainly archive photos, was not the same view that I was familiar with from using my own collection of photos as an area of reference, that is, some thousands of photos snapped by the average German *Landser*. It followed, then, that a book of photos relying heavily on the most dramatic and detailed official photos was not an honest representation of the time, the place or the people who took part in these events, nor, more importantly, how they saw themselves.

In this book are many photos that were taken by the rank and file German soldiers. Some of these photos I obtained directly from former members of the *Afrikakorps* living in Germany, while other photos came from the New Zealand and Australian returned servicemen who originally picked them up as souvenirs on the North African battlefields — including those photos that had been brought to Africa from home in Germany, as well as ones snapped in Africa. These personal photos, once owned by German soldiers, joined all the other war mementoes collected by Allied troops. The photos were removed from rucksacks and from pockets on the clothing of prisoners (and in some instances from corpses), taken from captured tanks, trucks and cars, from abandoned weapon sites, trenches and foxholes, all the way from El Alamein to Enfidaville.

These personal photos give a much truer overall view of their owners' army life, at the private and individual level of experience and of the war in North Africa, as seen by the average German soldier. The photos record how these men saw each other, and what they felt was important enough in the world around them to put on film. Those snapshots taken earlier in Germany and carried across the Mediterranean reveal common backgrounds of home life, and the face of German society in the Third Reich. Many of these photos show their former owners as members of such organisations as the Hitler Youth, the Stormtroopers, or the State Labour Service, and taking part in the parades and rallies that were a normal part of life in Hitler's Germany.

The information contained in the photos often illustrates small things that may not seem important in themselves but do say something about the personalities and attitudes of the soldiers involved: for instance, many men preferred wearing their tropical pith helmets back to front, a sensible modification as the wider rear rim gave better shade to the face. In the many photos taken in and around camps it is extremely rare to see any personal weapons, the small arms all soldiers were issued with, as one would have expected if the photos had been taken in Europe. Obviously, it was not expected that a raiding party of the enemy would suddenly appear from out of the desert. In Africa there were no partisans (if one excepts the occasional Arab sniper or the LRDG who ranged far in the rear) and the fighting usually took place along organised if moving lines of combat, involving mostly motorised artillery and tanks rather than large number of infantry, as was still the case in Europe at the time. What was seen around the tents and vehicles in camp scenes were trenches and rock-walled sangars built for protection against air attack. (In the event of a ground attack it would be more likely that the first reaction would be to jump into the nearest vehicle to get away as quickly as possible, not to jump into a trench to defend what was only, after all, a map reference.)

For those photos that can be placed at a certain location at a specific time there is information one can deduce, knowing the context of time and place. We see, for example, that even during the heaviest of battles, such as at El Alamein in October and November 1942, soldiers out of the front line stood around talking during mealtime, and that the usual routines of army life went on largely unaffected by the battle raging nearby. The battle itself did not reach out to disrupt the lives of those who were not actually engaged in the front line fighting, and for those men stationed behind the line their daily duties went on much as normal if at a faster tempo.

Cameras could not close the distance across which most of the fighting in North Africa took place. Wide angle and telephoto lenses (for detailed close-up and distant views) were not fitted to personal cameras. Only after the tide of battle had passed could close-up photos be taken of disabled or knocked-out tanks and other vehicles, groups of prisoners, enemy dead, and the debris of modern war that always littered the battlefields later.

Photos taken in Africa by German soldiers are not, of course, a totally accurate reflection of their day-to-day lives. Film was not always readily available and this meant that it was more likely to be used taking photos of the unusual and extraordinary, rather than the more mundane scenery and events — though this side of daily existence received its share of photos, too, for want of anything else to shoot with a camera.

In the same way that the official army photographers arranged shots to show 'battle' scenes, some German soldiers did the same thing to simulate in a photo the appearance and feel of battle. These photos were snapped after first arranging specially posed scenes with weapons for a suitable 'combat' backdrop. Of all the things that one would wish to record on film, it was that one most dangerous and memorable act — actual fighting — that was most difficult to photograph. Therefore, instead of real life battle scenes, the posed shots had to make do instead. Such photos, taken by ordinary soldiers, show to what extent the official view sanctioned by state propaganda and commonly seen in magazines and newspapers — essentially a romantic view of war as a heroic game — was accepted without irony by some soldiers as a real and serious record of themselves at war (and what would presumably be shown as part of one's personal war history later at home to family and friends).

The range of subjects covered in captured film and photos picked up on the battlefields was restricted by the type of military unit their previous owners had belonged to. Advancing troops were unlikely to overrun the rear base units of a motorised opposing army as these troops were invariably long gone by the time their former living and work areas were occupied. Thus, the majority of German soldiers who had their film and photos captured by the advancing enemy usually belonged to those who served in or near the front line — infantry, engineers, artillery, Flak and Pak gunners, and tank or reconnaissance units. Soldiers in these formation were, naturally enough, the ones most likely to lose their personal possessions, and their lives, in the fighting. Therefore, the majority of the photos reproduced in these pages are those that belonged to combat soldiers of the *Afrikakorps*, and not the men who served in any of the multitude of units stationed behind the lines. In this collection of photos I have not bothered to separate the Luftwaffe from the Army; both served, after all, as frontline soldiers in the one army in Africa.

To find photos showing the work and living areas of the rear support units, one has to go either to the official collections housing photos taken by wartime army photographers, or track down the surviving members of these rear units, or their children, living in Germany. In the German army in North Africa in World War II, there were roughly two soldiers serving in the frontline combat units for every one soldier behind the lines in some sort of rear support role. (For the Allied armies in North Africa, the ratio of frontline troops to rear support units ran the opposite way, with slightly more numerical strength in the rear area than in the combined frontline combat units.)

The scenes from this other war zone, often far behind the front lines, have received little attention in books covering the war. In addition to the view of the frontline area with which we are already familiar, with its combat vehicles and trenches, makeshift tents and foxholes, artillery and anti-tank guns with their piles of ammunition ready for use, there was an even more extensive area stretching out far behind the lines where a large number of the *Afrikakorps* carried out their duties. There were firstly the thousands of motor vehicles and their drivers who daily criss-crossed the desert roads and tracks, transporting everything from petrol and ammunition to cigarettes and vitamin pills up to the front; there were the large networks of supply dumps and their attendant staffs; extensive mechanical engineering workshops, complete with furnaces, welding gear and panel-beating equipment; the motor repair centres were numerous, with their well-equipped lorry-borne workshops and large compressors to provide the air pressure for blasting sand and dirt from engine parts, and gantries for lifting engine blocks in and out of vehicles; workshops permanently set up with heavy lathes and tools capable of rebuilding a wide range of mechanical equipment; paint shops where the innumerable roadside tactical signs were made up; there were carpenters' workshops, too, where thousands of tables, chairs and benches were made; Engineer companies busy rebuilding roads and erecting or repairing harbour facilities and setting up defensive fortifications; large bakeries cooking bread for thousands of men; there were Flak units guarding the ports; the Luftwaffe had meteorological units whose job it was daily to send high altitude balloons into the atmosphere to measure wind speeds and their moisture content and who travelled far and wide in the desert with their vehicles carrying tanks of compressed hydrogen; there was, in addition, the bureaucracy of the German army which followed it to North Africa, and these clerks in uniform worked busily from one end of Libya and Egypt to the other and finally across to Tunisia, creating on the way a small mountain of paper. There were other units as diverse as military police, meat butchery companies, units detailed for POW guard duties, military postal companies running mail sorting operations as large a one would find in a modern city; entertainers in the propaganda companies, tailors with their sewing machines mending uniforms, cobblers fixing boots, water purification units, hospitals and their staffs of nurses and doctors, dentists; ordnance companies whose job it was to service and repair weapons, journalists who produced the *Afrikakorps*' own newspaper, and so on. The photographic story of this other face of the *Afrikakorps* must wait for another book.

This book is, above all, a story in photographs of the men of the fighting units of the *Afrikakorps*, even though little of the fighting itself appears in the photos. Whether attempts to capture on film something of the true face of battle were made by amateur or professional photographers, the results were invariably the same — clouds on the horizon caused by the smoke rising from burning vehicles or from the columns of dust-filled air thrown up by exploding artillery shells. Whenever the battle moved much closer than the horizon, using their cameras was hardly the thought uppermost in the minds of the amateur photographer soldiers. The more common type of photo taken on the days when fighting had taken place showed groups of comrades snapped after the battle had passed, their faced showing the elation of survival and victory, or fatigue from what had been a period of great physical and emotional strain.

I have yet to see a photo taken by ordinary German soldiers of their own dead as they fell in battle, or any photo showing a comrade in death. (The official photographers did take shots of German dead.) For the average soldier it was common enough to snap the enemy dead, and funeral services and the graves of one's own comrades, but not the faces of the corpses of your own side. It was the same for Allied soldiers. It was as if the images of these deaths frozen in private memories were enough to last a lifetime.

As much as possible, the photos selected for reproduction here are ones that show the ordinary and common-place view of the world seen by the average soldier in the *Afrikakorps*. (To preserve the authenticity of these photos I have had to ask the people who produce this book not to clean up prints that at first seem dirty and 'spotty' — what look like grains of dirt printed from a filthy negative are most likely only flies.)

For the soldiers of the *Afrikakorps*, this was their world, its sights and faces. Much has been written about the war in North Africa since these photos were taken. As is the nature of history, our understanding of the events and of the period itself gradually changes as we look back from the ever-moving mood of the present. Time softens the lingering effects of the emotion-charged propaganda from the wartime years, and facts become easier to separate from what was invented, both at the time and later. Although stories of the war will alter with the passing of time, these photos will always remain unchanged, a timeless personal record.

Very little of the great volume of military stores transported across the Mediterranean by the German army from February 1941 to May 1943 now survives. Many of the photos taken during this period have also now disappeared. More than 20,000 German soldiers lie buried in North Africa, some of this number in unmarked and unknown graves. They deserve to be remembered, as do the dead of all armies.

Given the origin of many of these photos, picked up on the battlefield, many of their owners, the faces on these pages, will be among those who fell in Africa and whose bodies lie buried there today. It is my hope that readers will feel their imagination has been touched by something they see in one or more photos in these pages, and give it meaning.

FATHERLAND

Most German troops took photos to Africa that belonged to that part of their lives outside military service and before the war, photos that said much about who they were and where they came from. These photos illustrated life in the Germany of the 1930s and early 1940s, its towns and villages and countryside, its political, social and historical cultural identity.

While much Allied reporting of the war referred to German troops as 'Nazis', it was not a fair and accurate description of the average German soldier. There was little among the range of souvenirs collected by Allied troops that would have led one to believe the *Afrikakorps* was made up of 'Nazis'. There were of course photos that showed their owners as once belonging to Nazi organisations like the Hitler Youth and the State Labour Service, but this was obligatory for all young men in Hitler's Germany, and did not mean everyone had therefore become a 'Nazi'. The swastika clasped inside the talons of the eagles worn on German army caps and tunics was at the time the German national emblem, and did not in itself make individual soldiers 'Nazis'. If one looked for evidence among souvenirs for some indication of personal beliefs, one would probably conclude much of the *Afrikakorps* was from a Christian society. The *Afrikakorps* included military chaplains amongst its personnel, and many German soldiers, especially the Catholics who came mainly from the southern states and the Rhineland, carried various religious items among their personal effects, including bibles and prayer books. The men of the *Afrikakorps* were soldiers, no different from the soldiers of other armies of the period, under the same sort of military discipline, and with the same intense patriotism.

Wartime Allied propaganda deliberately, and very effectively, confused the political and social morality (or immorality) of the Nazi state with the personal and cultural morality and values of the individual German. The two were, in fact, not the same, except in a relatively small number of cases. Although some German soldiers serving in Africa were ardent Nazis (more so the younger soldiers and a smaller number of officers, if their behaviour in POW camps is taken into account), they were a small minority within the *Afrikakorps*. The German army at this time was not a 'Nazi' organisation in the sense that the SS was a Nazi organisation, nor was it committed to the goals of the Nazi state as was the *Luftwaffe*. The much older tradition of the German army, an imperial tradition with its values still firmly set in the *Kaiserreich,* was at this time strong enough to resist many of the political values espoused by the Nazi state. Only in the last year of the war did the German army accept the primary place of the party in its ranks, in the wake of the bomb plot of 20 July 1944. The greatest motivation for ordinary soldiers fighting in Africa was a pure and simple nationalism, albeit a Prussian sort of nationalism, militaristic and jingoistic. Reading through files of unit records from the period, or the letters written by soldiers and their families, one is struck today by the ordinary things that were talked about, not the 'Nazism' of Allied wartime propaganda with which the whole German population was painted. Postcards and photos of Hitler were often collected by Allied soldiers looking for souvenirs, but in the absence of other specific or general 'Nazi' literature one must assume that the photos of the Fuehrer were carried more to mark the charismatic 'leader' figure rather than the political ideology of the Nazi party. There is no doubt Hitler was idolised by a very large majority of soldiers at this early stage of the war. However, apart from the Hitler postcard portraits there was very little, if anything, that one could point to as explicitly representing 'Nazi ideology' among the personal possessions taken from German POWs in Africa.

Wartime German propaganda was very forcefully and cleverly communicated, and it was no different for German troops in Africa. This propaganda was an effective blend of Nazi ideology and straight patriotism, all wrapped up inside the familiar military virtues of honour, obedience and sacrifice. This propaganda reached the ordinary soldier through daily army orders, letters from home (where news stories were repeated verbatim), through newspapers and magazines sent from home, in movies seen in Africa, in radio broadcasts from Germany, and in their own local army newspaper, 'The Oasis', reporting information received from official sources in Germany.

Some soldiers, especially officers, carried with them to Africa items from World War I that had once belonged to their fathers, and with some of the older officers, such things were the very same items they had used themselves in that war — binoculars, pistols, leather map cases etc. Even photos of scenes in World War I were found among the private papers carried to Africa by some soldiers. Presumably these military shots were personal and family ones, but they showed that the nature of war had changed little, only the scenery and weaponry were different.

From newspapers, and the postmarks on letters and postcards picked up along with the photos (which provided information on the origins of the photos), there was a strong local flavour in 1941 for the original two divisions of the *Afrikakorps,* Berlin, Potsdam, Görlitz, Wünsdorf, Western Silesia for 5th Light Div, and the Upper Rhineland and Swabia for 15th Panzer Div. By the end of 1941 the local geographical flavour associated with the first two divisions of the *Afrikakorps* was diluted. It began with the creation of the 90th Light Div. (which had in its ranks many former members of the French Foreign Legion who came from every corner of Germany) and the other divisions that arrived in 1942 and 1943 included many Saxons, Austrians, men from other parts of Prussia, and Bavarians, and so on. The practice of taking replacements from other parts of Germany for the original divisions drew in new areas as well. By the second half of 1942, most geographical areas of Germany were represented in the *Afrikakorps.*

If German soldiers had only their photos to remind them of their homeland, it must have been a very idealised view — family picnics in the countryside, weekend gatherings with family and friends, holiday snaps, homes, civilian jobs, sweethearts, children... When looking at such tranquil peacetime scenes as these photos today, there is a sense of unreality about their more recent origins in burnt-out tanks and vehicles, in foxholes and trenches, in the North African desert in the middle of a war.

A German soldier snapped during the First World War, a photo found among the personal belongings of German POWs in Bardia in January 1942.

...arade in the pre-war years of the uniformed German Labour front, the Nazified trade union movement.

One of the many postcards of Adolf Hitler carried to Africa by German soldiers in 1941 and 1942.

Parade of Stormtroopers, the brown-shirted para-military arm of the Nazi Party.

Family shot. The uniform
worn second from left is RAD
(Reichsarbeitsdienst) State
Labour Service.

The Brown House, the Nazi
Party HQ of the 1920s and
1930s in Munich.

In RAD uniform.

RAD camp, wooden huts in the pine forests.

RAD service.

Six female members of the RAD.

Not all time in the RAD was spent in hard work.

Night shot of young members from an unknown paramilitary organisation on a training camp before the war.

Gymnasts drawn from a Panzer Regiment practice their routines for a military display.

An army band prepares for a weekend concert.

THE ARMY IN EUROPE, AT HOME AND AT WAR

P hotos dealing with German military service before Africa were of great interest to the Allied troops who acquired them. The photos seemed to answer questions about the origins or ancestry of the *Afrikakorps*, to make real the imaginings of Allied soldiers about just who it was over the other side of the hill. In fact, the *Afrikakorps* were only ordinary German troops, in spite of the different tropical uniforms, and their elementary training at least was little different from that which the Allied soldiers themselves had received.

Most groups of photos removed from POWs and other sources found on the battlefield included at least a few showing military service in Europe before being posted to Africa. Many of these photos were taken at army bases during basic training, the six months done by those who had joined after the outbreak of war. The DAK in 1941 however was a mixture of the professional soldiers from the pre-war army, and young conscripts or volunteers who had joined the army after the outbreak of war. The German divisions arriving in Africa after 1941, and the later reinforcement drafts, consisted increasingly of rank and file men who had joined up in wartime.

For the younger generation of soldiers in the *Afrikakorps* their military education had started while still adolescents with the Hitler Youth, and continued with the RAD (State Labour Service) and the other paramilitary organisations all young Germans were encouraged to join. Their time in the army was seen thus as the normal progression towards more specialised military training, something expected of all young German males.

n of Panzer Regiment 5
he Winter of 1939-40.

While the German army's basic training may have been similar in most respects to that which other armies gave their recruits, German military tactics were the most progressive, and the most modern, in the world at that time. For the individual soldier this emphasised one's overall military function inside a moving battle with its mechanised units and two-way radios joining up units with each other on the battlefield and with the *Luftwaffe* planes in close support. Most Allied armies still taught a more narrow and singular arm of service training (reminiscent of World War I) and hence fast co-operation between these arms of service was missing on the battlefield. The German 'all arms' training gave its commanders the confidence to undertake the penetration attacks with armour deep into enemy territory, ignoring old fixations with secure lines of supply and cover for the flanks at all costs. The training *Afrikakorps* soldiers were given led to their ability to fight easily and surely in close co-operation with all other arms of service, always aggressively counter-attacking immediately when put under attack. The 'Battle Groups' that were made up as mixtures of component parts of available units were to become just as familiar as the old established units. Above all, it was the abiding high morale of these soldiers, and the professionalism of officers young and old, ready converts to the new tactics of mechanised and armoured war, *Blitzkrieg,* that carried the new doctrine of modern warfare so forcefully to their enemy in Africa.

The campaigns in Poland and France were seen in these captured photos too, and even scenes of the Eastern Front on Soviet territory found their way to North Africa in 1942 and 1943.

A new barracks, one of so many such built for the *Wehrmacht* in the 1930s.

'The soldier', aiming a small pistol for a very posed photo.

Horse drawn transport through a Sudeten village in September 1938 as Hitler incorporates the German-speaking part of Czechoslovakia into the Reich.

Basic training, hauling the 15cm *schwere Feldhaubitze* 18, the heavy field howitzer of the German Army, Erfurt 1940.

Anonymous personal shot taken some time over 1939–1940 and found near Fort Capuzzo in late 1941.

By the River Rhine, late summer 1940.

Basic training Erfurt 1940, climbing down ropes suspended from the ceiling, wearing the stuffy gasmask.

Ramming the shell into the breech of the heavy 15cm howitzer in basic training for these artillery recruits, Erfurt 1940.

1939, war in Poland, German panzers of PzRgt5 in a Polish village.

PzII of PzRgt5 in the Polish campaign.

Men of a Luftwaffe Flak unit being addressed on their barracks parade ground by the commanding officer on the eve of departure.

Home leave for a young soldier in early 1941, brother and sister.

Farewell to Germany – the mountains of Austria and Bavaria, snapped through train windows in 1941. For many German soldiers, this was to be their last view of Germany.

TRANSIT: GOODBYE GERMANY, HELLO AFRICA

Before departure for Africa there was normally a home leave, seven to ten days in 1941 but reduced to a shorter time by 1943 of three or four days only. Photos taken on these last home visits were carried on their person by many troops in Africa. For the first main units to leave Germany in 1941, the 5th Light Division, and *Luftwaffe* Flak *Abteilungen,* there were formal farewell parades on barrack squares surrounded by snow-covered buildings, a ceremonial send-off that was not repeated after 1941. A similar atmosphere of occasion and ceremony awaited them in Tripoli, endless columns of tanks rattling down main thoroughfares, straight lines of troops standing waiting for inspection by Rommel and the Italian General Garibaldi.

In direct violation of orders that all photographs were to be taken away from POWs (for their alleged intelligence value), it was common for some kindly Allied soldiers to leave snapshots of family groups with their German POW owners (and just as common for other Allied captors to regard these private snapshots as another interesting and rightful souvenir for themselves).

Members of the 5th Light Division and 15th Panzer Division travelling through Rome in 1941 remember the NSDAP (Nazi Party) booths set up on the railway station, dispensing food and drinks to trainloads of troops passing through. These refreshment stalls were operated by German women whose husbands had diplomatic, military or commercial postings in Rome.

The very first troops from 5th Light Div. to arrive in Libya during February 1941 still wore their woollen continental uniforms. They were the first and the last troops to do so. From March 1941 the German army issued its soldiers travelling to Africa with tropical uniform in Germany itself.

Those troops who travelled on to Africa by ship from Naples in 1941 had to wait for convoys to be arranged. This gave them time to do the usual tourist trips around Naples, and many photos were taken of the preserved Roman city of Pompeii and the lava flows below the slopes of Mt. Vesuvius.

Regardless of when and how he arrived in Africa, the German soldier carried his weapon with him and a canvas rucksack containing spare uniform and clothing items, along with his basic field equipment. The German army had to transport everything it needed to fight in Africa as there was nothing to be had locally to supplement its own resources. Absolutely everything had to be transported across the Mediterranean — food, vitamin pills, heavy and light weapons, ammunition, all vehicles and spare parts, fuel, typewriters, paper, soap, spare buttons, medical supplies, toilet paper, complete engineering workshops, thousands of kilometres of telephone cable, spare stocks of everything, literally everything... (hence the magnitude of the problems caused by high losses of supplies sunk crossing the Mediterranean).

After the summer of 1941, the most common route for troops travelling to Africa was by rail through the Balkans, then by aircraft from Greece or Crete to airfields in Libya. Photos taken in transit by *Afrikakorps* soldiers in 1941 and 1942 show a variety of backyard views of cities and towns stretching from Berlin to Naples and Taranto, from Vienna to Belgrade and Athens, snapped through train windows.

From the second half of 1941 many German soldiers spent long periods in Greece, waiting for transport across the Mediterranean to North Africa. By late 1941 tent cities had sprung up around Athens and the harbour at Piraeus. Photos dating from this time showed soldiers in tropical uniform, either singly or in groups, standing in front of a stone block wall and date palm trees. One candid street photographer in Athens did good business at this particular spot judging by the large number of photos taken against this one recognisably Mediterranean backdrop.

The new tropical uniform. Hans Schilling (on right) and friend stand in newly issued *Afrikakorps* uniform at Baumholder, June 1941.

Passing time in the warm sunshine in Naples in April 1941.

Unlike the reception given to troops arriving in Tripoli in 1941 who had crossed by sea, and were then handled by the well-established German military presence in this large city, things were very different in 1942. Nearly all reinforcements sent to Rommel in 1942 were flown in by the Luftwaffe to remote Libyan or Egyptian airfields from where they often had to make their own way to whatever unit they were assigned to. Transport was scarce, and fuel was even scarcer, and so it was that new arrivals had to move on with a minimum of help from the rear area units. It was usually up to the combat units to arrange vehicles to go back to the airfields to collect their own reinforcement drafts. Such organisational niceties that allowed reception facilities to be set up in Tripoli in 1941 were an extravagance in the desert war of 1942. There were no parades before the propaganda cameras for the steady trickle of troops arriving in the Ju52s at airfields such as Fuka, Derna, Gambut, El Adem and El Daba.

Reception in Tunisia for arriving troops was more in line with conditions then operating in Italy or Greece where there was a considerable German military presence, including all the usual rear support services. In Tunisia the German army was able to take over French army facilities, barracks and depots. In November 1942 Parachute Rgt5 paraded through the streets of Tunis, as a successful propaganda display, in a manner reminiscent of PzRgt5 in Tripoli in March 1941.

For some troops there was only a short stay in Africa, as dysentery struck down many who then had to be repatriated to hospitals in Europe. For those who fell in Africa — the 18,594 officially listed as killed, and 3,400 missing, it was a one-way journey.

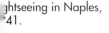

ghtseeing in Naples, '41.

The harbour dockside at Naples in 1941.

Cargo ship crane hoisting up a Volkswagen.

Passenger ships at Taranto in the summer of 1941.

anks of Panzer Regiment 5
on parade through Tripoli,
and taking the road to the
front in March 1941.

diterranean crossing.

A 10.5cm howitzer of Pz Art.Rgt 33 comes over the side and on to African soil.

Lined up for torpedo drill with kapok filled vests strapped on.

A Ford 3-ton truck of Pz Artl.Rgt 33 being unloaded in Tripoli.

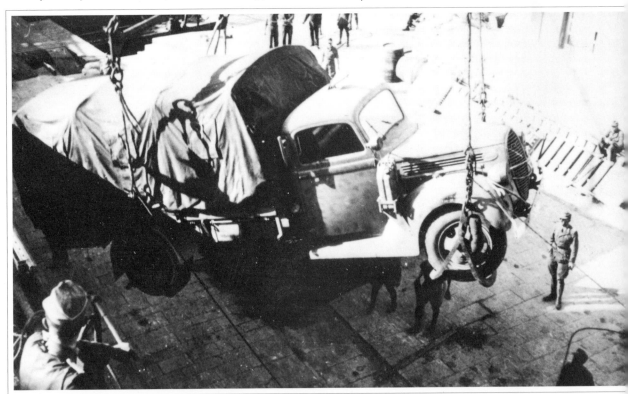

One of the many photos snapped by a Greek candid photographer who did good business in front of this wall and gate with the large palm trees behind.

Tripoli waterfront cafe, 1941.

In late 1941 and for most of 1942 the only safe way to reach Africa was by Junkers 52, as it was here for *Sonderverband* 288 in December 1941.

ew from Ju52 cockpit flying
across the Mediterranean.

ur photos from a spool of film taken by a member of a Flak unit that was sent from
rmany to Tunisia in early December 1942. The men in the photos, who are all from
one 88mm gun crew, are wearing their woollen European uniforms during this
st part of their journey. The photos were taken on a training base somewhere in
varia and on a train between Germany and the alps of Austria or Northern Italy.

Sidewalk cafe, Crete or Greece, 1941.

A group of men who had been lucky enough to get home leave in 1942 (or who had been sent back because of wounds) wait on an airfield in Crete for a flight to take them back to Egypt.

BEFORE AND AFTER

A common assortment of photos taken from POWs consisted of groups of photos showing their previous owners at various stages in their civilian and military careers. These photos taken from leather wallets and cardboard packets usually showed the man firstly as a civilian, later as a recruit in basic training and finally as a soldier of the *Afrikakorps*, marking out the milestones in the lives of these young German soldiers. The photos were very often large size studio portraits, wedding photos or pictures taken at the time of a home leave to show off a smart-looking new military uniform.

Studio shot,
Germany 1940.

Snapshot, Africa 1941.

Two photos of a member of 15th Pz Div, on his wedding day (with Hitler Youth badge on his left top pocket), and in the field, Africa 1941.

Two shots of a man who trained in 1942 and was sent to Tunisia with the 5th Panzer Army; in civilian dress (with Nazi Party badge in buttonhole) and in Tunis wearing tropical uniform with pistol on his belt.

eter Hellreigel in peace and
war, as a Hitler Youth, and
as a seasoned *Afrikaner*.
(Dieter Hellriegel)

The 'Arco dei Feleni', or Marble Arch, on the Via Balbia marking the boundary between Tripolitania and Cyrenaica, one of the most photographed features in Libya.

The border wire strung along the Libyan border with Egypt, intended to keep the troublesome Arab tribes from crossing from country to country.

A timeless scene, petrol being slowly siphoned from the van's tank into a tin containing sand, which will be flamed to burn under something heated up for lunch.

TYPICALLY AFRICAN

The scenery that met the soldiers of the *Afrikakorps* in Libya in 1941 was not what they had expected — the desert was often rocky instead of being smooth and sandy, and the German army had not prepared them for the day-to-day problems connected with desert-living health and hygiene. The oases so familiar from Hollywood movies were generally nowhere to be seen, and the swarms of flies came as an unpleasant surprise, as did the host of other insect pests. The German army had in fact done very little to prepare its soldiers for life in North Africa. Troops who arrived in 1942 and 1943 were somewhat better prepared for what awaited them, though this had more to do with a higher level of general awareness by everyone in the human supply pipeline rather than from any specially prepared instruction. It was the same for the whole units and the smaller reinforcement drafts sent over after 1941 — they continued to receive only the usual basic training meted out to all German recruits, regardless of where they were to serve. The official military attitude in 1942 and 1943 to North African service seemed to be that if the units sent over in 1941 had coped without any major preparation then so could the following reinforcements who would be instructed by the units already there.

Photos recording the popular romantic images of Africa were not as common in 1941 and 1942 from Libya and Egypt as they were later in Tunisia — of the Arabs themselves, date palms with camels and donkeys, Arab villages and mosques. Photos taken of Arabs in Tunisia were easier to get, because their villages were more numerous and closer to the main roads, and because the Tunisian Arabs were friendlier than those in Libya and Egypt. However, some of the few German soldiers who managed to get a closer view of Arab living conditions in Libya in 1941 and 1942 also recorded the poverty of the Arab villages, showing that not all Germans wished to photograph only the romantic movie images of Arab desert life.

The Mediterranean beaches were popular photo subjects, and not only as a backdrop for swimming parties. The Libyan (and Egyptian) beaches were more attractive looking to *Afrikakorps* soldiers than German Baltic and North Sea beaches and were so seen as worthwhile photo scenes in themselves.

Photography undertaken in the open desert was not easy, unless someone had a good camera and used it with the knowledge of how to compensate for the bright glare (to shoot away from it and so make use of it). Many shots taken in the desert were not successful, the brighter light meant the photos were often over-exposed and, in any case, it was difficult to capture any sense of scale and proportion for larger scenes when the horizon was just a hazy junction between shimmering desert and bright atmospheric light.

The absence in the desert of any of the features that distinguished the European landscape made any sort of landmark an important point from which one could get

CHAPTER 5

some bearings, a wrecked vehicle or tank for instance. Sometimes there were photos of insignificant pieces of wreckage that seem to have been photographed for no other reason than that they were some variation on the endless vista of desert from horizon to horizon, and something on a more familiar human scale. Photos showing the Via Balbia and vehicles were very common — this long asphalt ribbon with its heavy traffic was a sight known to every German soldier who served in North Africa in 1941 and 1942. Photos taken at or near areas that had been the scene of a battle invariably show the amazing amount of debris left by the fighting, literally everything in part or whole that had been carried there by soldiers, from bits of clothing to small personal items, from mess tins to petrol canisters and tyres, wrecked vehicles and weapons.

Some photos were taken of the arable areas in Libya, around Tripoli and in the hinterland to Benghazi where there was natural vegetation and some agriculture. That not more photos exist of these areas is explained by the short time German soldiers spent there — they were usually glimpsed only in transit with most time spent camped out in the open desert.

The old Roman ruins were always well photographed, and were popular places to visit, especially those at Leptis Magna, Apollonia, and Cyrene, which were the most accessible. For the professional as well as amateur photographers, the distinctive stone forts built mainly during the period Libya was occupied by Turkey, made another popular subject. These desert forts with their distinctive battlements, along with palm trees, camels and mosques, seemed to fit the popular image 1940s Europe had of the North African desert.

Another puncture, another r
Bardia. (Note that the tyre h

Typical of many 1941 photos
an expanse of desert, rocks a
Plateau.

Tapping artesian water with help from Arab villagers.

cross-country vehicle of 15 PzDiv, summer 1941, near
~~~ged as well as a wheel and tube.)

~~nding before
~~he Libyan

Dieter Hellriegel's photo of the most important African possessions — two
jerricans, paybook, his cloth field cap and two photos of his girlfriend, at El
Alamein September 1942. (Dieter Hellriegel)

The Mediterranean as bathing beaches.

45

The view from the bluff above the harbour at Bardia, 1941.

Der Spatengang (the walk with spade), heading off to a quiet spot with the necessary spade and a folded sheet of newspaper.

Arab villagers snapped in the hinterland of Benghazi in the summer of 1941.

Camels, face to face, 1941.

A sandstorm *(Ghibli)* rolls in from the desert towards
village on the Libyan coastal strip.

Flies, flies, flies, flies... here sucking up the perspirati
left on a steering wheel.

The arable belt of Libyan coastal land and Italian colonial farmhouses near Tigrinna.

...ater collection point from a
...l using an Italian lorry.

...shing in an irrigation
...e by a LW Flak unit.

Arab villager and *Luftwaffe* gunner, 1941.

Arab villager with an egg to trade, Bardia, 1941.

The main Bardia township above the harbour.

Waiting, 1941
Pz.Abw.Abt.39.

Morning wash, using the rationed little portion of water poured into the small
rubberised canvas folding 'bowl' all German soldiers in Africa were issued
with for this purpose.

Another function for the gasmask tin, as a seat.

51

Oft-photographed desert wreckage, such as this Italian Fiat CR42 biplane.

Desert navigation, using a compass.

Bomb crater next to an Italian
vehicle workshop near
Bardia in summer 1941.

Protection for tyres from the
hot sun.

The rear HQ bus of 15th Pz.Div. nearly afloat, caught in a wadi in flood after heavy rain near Tmimi on 17 February 1942. On top of the bus are Major (GS) von Loeffelholz, his aide *Oberleutnant* Karl-Heinz Böttger, and the *Gefreiter* who was its driver.

After driving through a sandstorm, *Oberleutnant* Karl-Heinz Böttger and the rear HQ bus of 15th Pz.Div. Both show signs of being coated with sand in April 1942.

...porting for orders, south of Tobruk in 1941.

A rare sight, a pet dog, Egypt 1942 (very likely brought across in an aircraft from Greece or Crete).

One of the soldiers' bars set up in the rear settlements along the Libyan coastal strip in 1941.

55

Rommel standing with Walter Fromm on the dockside in Tripoli, watching the first men and equipment of Pz.Abw.Abt.39 unloading on 14 February 1941. (Walter Fromm)

Rommel's *Luftwaffe* pilot holds the door back as a smiling Rommel prepares to get out.

Rommel on one of his many visits to frontline areas in 1941, here at Sollum with a party of German and Italian officers (the officer to the left with binoculars around his neck is Heinz Werner Schmidt, Rommel's ADC in 1941). (Charles Hinz)

ROMMEL

U ndoubtedly, Rommel was the most photographed person in North Africa between 1941 and 1943. The official German photographers followed him around and snapped him in many thousands of photos. The personal cameras of the ordinary soldier took many more thousands of photos.

Rommel was not averse to having his photo taken, and was known to have walked towards a person with a camera in their hands. He made an effort to be known by his soldiers, to be recognised by them on and off the battlefield, and to this end he always tried to show himself to his men.

It was not difficult to recognise Rommel, even though he invariably had a train of officers following behind him. For most of the time he wore the woollen continental Generals' service cap with its high crown and silvered insignia, and there were always the distinctive lightweight British anti-gas goggles worn around the cap. His other uniform was no less distinctive, a long olive-tan leather greatcoat, or the tailor-made cotton tropical uniform quite different in cut to the normal army issue tunic, and he usually wore high black leather boots. Rommel had a characteristic stance when talking to someone, to plant his legs slightly apart and his head cocked to one side, a posture that was soon well known.

Rommel with the Italian General Gariboldi in Tripoli on 4 March 1941, about to review newly arrived German troops.

Rommel showed real concern for the welfare of his soldiers, and they knew it. He did not lose the common touch and always felt at ease talking with rank and file troops. The soldiers realised that the very strict rules affecting their daily existence ordered by Rommel were in their best interest. Very simply, they believed in him.

Many German soldiers saw him fleetingly during the fighting as he arrived standing in his staff car to check dispositions rapidly and urge on his junior commanders before driving off at speed to some other part of the battlefield. He had a terse style of giving commands and expected his officers to jump to their tasks as soon as he had finished giving instructions.

Rommel's shoulder straps for a General were silver/gold-coloured twisted braid with silver pips over a red felt underlay. After the fall of Tobruk, he wore the crossed batons of a Field Marshal on his shoulder straps.

Rommel also took his share of photos while in Africa and he was often to be seen with his Leica case unbuttoned and camera ready for an interesting shot. Sadly, many of these photos taken by Rommel did not survive the war.

Rommel receives a high Italian decoration during a visit to an Italian HQ in the late summer of 1941.

Italian submarine that had
supplies into Bardia while
was cut off by the British
vance in June 1941
ceived a visit by Rommel,
o was given a glass of
ne by the captain.

ith Hauptmann the
verend Wilhelm Bach (at
) and members of 1st
ttalion Inf.Rgt.104 (mot) at
lfaya in July 1941.

Obviously pleased with his visit, Rommel smiles as he prepares to leave, and one Italian officer makes a formal bow.

The *Chef* arrives in his personal Fieseler *Storch* (Stork).

ROMMEL

A postcard that was available in the second half of 1942, taken in very early 1942, with Italian decorations prominently showing. (This photo was taken six months or so before he had been promoted to Field Marshal, in spite of the card's caption.)

Rommel on the cliff above Bardia Harbour with the Italian submarine he had just visited visible in the bay below.

A typical impromptu conference around Rommel's *Horch* in September 1942, with officers from Pz.Gren.Rgt 200 at El Alamein. The officer sitting in the back with Rommel is Colonel Baylerlein.

61

A permanent lavatory was used outside this camp near Bardia in the summer of 1941 – a 44-gallon drum half buried in the ground with a board placed on top of the open upper end.

The common way of lowering the daytime heat inside a tent was to rig a second canvas skin above the actual tent to make an insulated layer of cooler air between the two canvas surfaces.

CAMP SCENES

T he usual accommodation for German troops living in the open desert consisted of various sized canvas tents. Often these tents were pitched two at a time, a larger tent over a smaller one with the space between them giving some insulation from the searing heat of the sun. Whenever the ground was not too hard, the tent tops could be erected above pits dug into the sand. This gave effective cover against enemy bombs and artillery fire (unless there was a direct hit). If the ground was too hard to dig into, tents could be slung alongside vehicles which provided some protection and shade, or surrounded by low mounds of rocks (sangars). The tents were always well dispersed, with tents and vehicles spread out across the desert to minimise the risk of heavy damage from air attack by presenting a large number of separated small targets instead of larger clusters of targets. It was usual for foxholes, or slit trenches, to be dug close to tents if time allowed. Few German soldiers were ever fortunate enough to pitch their tents for any length of time inside an oasis, with its shady date palms and abundant fresh water.

A special treat on Adolf Hitler's birthday for these members of 15th Panzer Division recently arrived in Libya, a three course meal served up after making camp on the evening of 20 April 1941.

The usual objects scattered around all campsites were jerricans (especially the ones with the white cross on the sides used for water only), wooden and metal ammunition boxes which served as outdoor seating, and the simple wooden tables and chairs made in the army's own carpentry shops in the rear. Nearby there were usually trenches or rocky sangars for use in the event of an air attack. The chimneys of the German army kitchen on wheels, the 'Goulash Cannon', were likely to be sited near the larger and more permanent camps. In smaller and frontline living areas meals were transported in insulated containers from a central kitchen, or were cooked and warmed up over small fires by men remote from permanent kitchens. Petrol poured over sand in a tin and then lit was a popular method of making a fire to warm one's meal.

Only a few photos recorded the mundane and routine scenes that were repeated many, many times, a soldier sewing on a button or sleeve insignia for example, or the means by which uniforms were cleaned — woollen overcoats were brushed to remove sand and dirt, while the cotton uniforms items of cap, tunic, shirt and trousers were washed in petrol or seawater and then rubbed with clean dry sand (unless soap was available to rub into the dirtiest patches).

Personal weapons were only rarely seen in photos of campsites, and even the heavier weapons like artillery or tanks were normally sited some distance away from the tents. Larger and more permanent campsites with caravans or buses like battalion or regimental HQs were normally well camouflaged, using the abundant camelthorn bushes to break up the familiar outline of vehicles.

Wadis were popular places for campsites too, but there was always the risk that a flash storm out in the desert would sent a torrent of water down the wadi. Hence most camps put up in a wadi were more likely to be for a short time only.

Camps were often dotted with signposts, both the official army tactical identification signs and the unofficial ones that counted the distance in kilometres to Berlin, or advertised such and such a site as the 'beautiful tropical holiday resort of the 104th Infantry Regiment' etc.

Campsites always meant time for a haircut.

Regular chore, washing underclothes and socks.

Paul Erich Schläfer sews a button on his woollen
greatcoat, November 1941.

Four camouflage shelter
quarters have here been
joined on the back of a
anomen truck in a camp
ar Bardia in the summer
of 1941.

65

This collection of signs at the entrance to a camp includes one warning that mines are ahead, another advertising tourist trips to 'beautiful Germany' (*Besucht das schöne Deutschland*) and the bottom sign advises that here is a 'track' for cyclists only.

These three men have unloaded their cargo of water jerricans to arrange protective walls to sleep inside for the night.

A tent home in the desert for members of 15th PzDiv south of Bardia in the summer of 1941.

...ngsten (Whitsun) 1941
...RIKA — place and unit
...nown.

...e personal staff of the
...geon-General of the
...ikakorps at their campsite
...der the palms near
...surata in March 1942.

Beside a trench dug to give protection against air attack,
2nd Company *Sonderverband* 288 in the summer of 1942.

The company tailor with his table-top treadle-operated Singer
sewing machine. The *Afrikakorps* tailors were busy prolonging the
life of uniforms when supplies were not reaching North Africa.

Mass being celebrated for members of the Pioneer Battalion in
15thPzDiv in the summer of 1941.

Photograph showing shelters dug into the ground and covered with canvas and sand used by members of a Flak unit south of Tobruk in 1941.

‑up that accompanied
embers of Rommel's
gleitkommando in late
41 .
ieter Hellriegel)

Photo taken to record visit
from Arab villagers who
arrived with eggs and dates
to sell.

Franz Seidl, 2nd Company
Sonderverband 288, June 1942.

Unteroffizier, from Rommel's *Begleitkommando,*
Wadi Matratin November 1941.
(Dieter Hellriegel)

FACES

The faces of the German soldiers in the photos on these pages are from individual snapshots taken in Africa, studio portraits taken in Europe, family snapshots, and the official ID photos removed from the soldier's army service passbook *(Wehrpass)*. Except in those instances where the photos were obtained from original owners still living today, no names are known. These other photos are identified only by their origin, taken by Allied soldiers from German POWs and abandoned positions in North Africa in World War II.

They need no captions. In reply to the question, "Who were the *Afrikakorps*?" there is one simple answer. They are the faces in these photos.

oya, summer of 1941,
areheaded member of
15Pz Divisional staff.

Leutnant Wolfgang Doering, Rommel's *Begleitkommando* (Escort unit) in November 1941. (Dieter Hellriegel)

Oberzahlmeister Schmidt, Staff Company, Rommel's *Kampfstaffel,* El Alamein, 1942. (Dieter Hellriegel)

Panzer crewman, showing the special black woollen uniform worn by tankers in Europe, photo found in a knocked out tank near Tobruk in December 1941.

Prewar studio shot of a member of 21PzDiv as civilian.

In Basic Training, Erfurt 1941.

Oberschirrmeister Förderreuter, Staff Company, Rommel's *Kampfstaffel*, El Alamein, 1942. (Dieter Hellriegel)

73

Three members of 2nd Company, *Sonderverband* 288, June 1942.

2nd Company, *Sonderverband* 288, 1942.

Member of 2nd MG Battalion (5th Light Div.)

Feldwebel from a *Luftwaffe* Flak unit.

Small souvenir, a photo torn from a captured military driving licence by an Australian soldier at El Alamein.

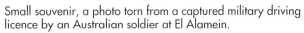

Luftwaffe Signaller, wearing the Italo-German African Campaign Medal on his left pocket.

Leutnant Barisch, Adjutant
Fla.Btln 606 early 1942.

Hans Schilling, studio shot during basic training in early 1941.

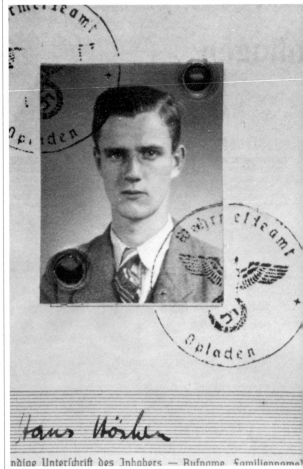

Johannes Höschen, born 1920 in
Düsseldorf, in 1941 he served in
Afrika-Rgt 361, 90th Light Division
(Wehrpass photo).

Leutnant, Paratrooper and qualified glider pilot, two snaps taken in Europe before serving in Africa.

Hauptmann Georg Briel, CO of Fla.Btln 606 in early 1942.

CHAPTER 8

Unknown members Fla/Btln 606 in winter 1942.

With Iron Cross 2nd Class ribbon and General Assault badge, Private rank.

Officer, *Oberleutnant,* with cigar and wearing pith helmet.

Pith helmet and privately acquired sweater.

Unknown faces from Pz/GrenRgt 200 snapped by Georg Briel around the time just before the El Alamein Battle in October 1942.

Hauptfeldwebel, wearing the State Award for Physical Training Badge.

Oberleutnant, Company Commander, with Iron Cross 1st Class and the General Assault Badge.

Officer (by silver cording on cap), rank unknown.

Officer (by silver cording on cap), rank unknown.

Grenadier (infantry private rank).

Unflinching, as flies crawl over mouth and nostrils, this grenadier stands stiffly to attention as Major Briel awards an Iron Cross 1st Class in September 1942.

faces of Georg Briel in August 1942.
waffe, Flak gunner, *Kanonier* (Private rank).

Photo taken from wallet found at Belhammed, November 1941.

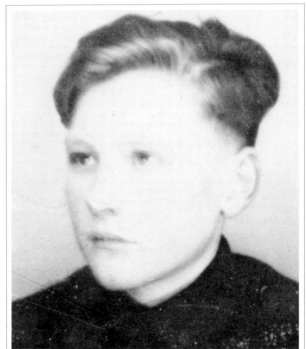

Typical assortment of rations for three days in the early months of 1942 for a *Zug* (platoon) of 2nd Company *Sonderverband* 288 — loaves of bread from the regimental bakery, tins of Italian sausage meat and Norwegian sardines in olive oil, oranges, tubes of cheese (in the cloth sacks) and a few tins of ersatz coffee and sugar.

Rations being handed out on the Egyptian border on 3rd May 1941, a dollop of fruit conserve into the lid of the mess tin and two oranges.

FOOD AND DRINK

No German soldier who served in North Africa could ever forget the standard diet as provided by the army — processed cheese in tube containers, tinned sardines in olive oil, Italian military issue tinned sausage meat (the infamous 'AM'), German Dauerbrot (a wholesome and popular moist long lasting bread, made from 'black' rye or wheat, and wrapped in foil), the occasional fresh wholemeal bread, onions and dehydrated vegetables (legumes), an oatmeal gruel, the hard and dry Italian army biscuits, and whatever captured food was available (always seen as the ultimate luxury by German troops bored with their own rations).

The staple drink was usually purified water — heavy with chemical agents — and drunk as reconstituted lemon 'juice' or as *ersatz* coffee (a synthetic substitute for coffee), which still tasted of the chemicals added to make the water suitable for human consumption. What water was not used for drinking or cooking had to stretch to cover shaving and washing, cleaning teeth, and for rinsing out socks, singlets and underpants.

It was normal practice for the *Wehrmacht* to issue vitamin tablets to its soldiers as a dietary supplement, a policy actively encouraged by Hitler who believed in the power of vitamins to improve one's health and well-being. British Intelligence officers in the 8th Army, whose job it was to analyse all captured German material, including food stores, showed amazement when cartons of vitamin pills were discovered among German stores in Libya in November and December 1941. Stories of these then relatively uncommon pills used by the *Afrikakorps* gave rise to stories in wartime Allied press that the German soldiers in Africa were some sort of new twentieth century Aryan supermen, using drugs *(sic)* to increase their physical strength.

he exception, a formal -down meal served up to German and Italian officers from the Rear Army Command in Benghazi in 1941.

However, the average German soldier envied the diet of their enemy. By common agreement in the *Afrikakorps* the most delicious food in the desert was captured from the enemy — tinned corned beef and fresh white bread, followed closely by tinned fruits, especially peaches, apricots and pineapple. The issue of German gastronomic delights from the homeland such as ham, beer and sausage, fresh potatoes, and sweets such as chocolate, were rare events. American army food captured in Tunisia caused acute envy among German troops also.

The only regular supplementary food available to the *Afrikakorps* (apart from captured stores) either came from home, the occasional fruitcake sent by families through the post, or what was obtained from local Arabs. Whenever it was possible to trade with Arab villagers food was always at the top of the list — eggs, chickens, fruit, tomatoes and fresh dates.

Efforts by so-called 'experts' in nutrition in Berlin who sent a stream of advice to units in Africa aimed at improving the standard diet were usually wildly out of touch with reality. One such official pronouncement circulated through the 5th Light Division in May 1941 contained a recipe for a 'nutritious liquid snack suitable for times when on the move', consisting of a mixture of the following ingredients: '$1/_2$ liter water; $1/_2$ tube cordial; 30gr marmalade; 30-35gr sugar; 30gr groats or rice.

Like any army, Germany soldiers in Africa were pre-occupied with their stomachs and what went into them. Food was a popular subject of conversation (especially for the black humour of soldiers), even if the fare itself was not popular. Many of the photos taken by *Afrikakorps* men were to do with eating, and with the preparation of food.

The standard German diet was a constant source of concern, for the soldiers forced to eat it, and the supply units who were unable to substitute it with anything more wholesome or tasty.

A common scene at the time of the midday meal, gathered around the cookhouse truck with the usual collection of water jerricans. Sign on the back door reads 'Entry Forbidden' *(Eintritt verboten!)*

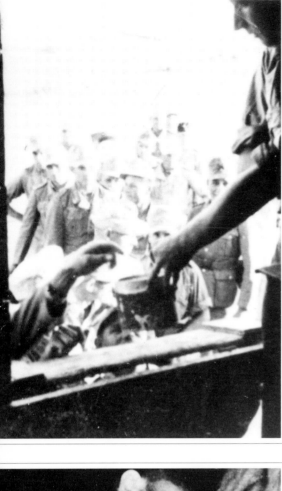

Three shots taken by a cook of a special meal, which included fresh meat, being prepared in the summer of 1941.

The end result: serving up portions in the proferred mess tins of the company.

One of the cooks slicing pork.

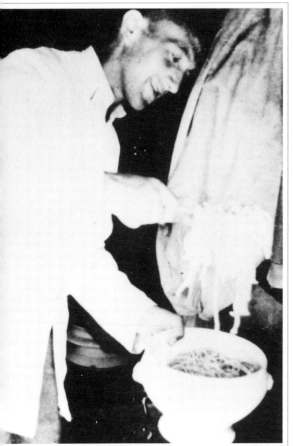

A bowl of noodles being tossed inside the cookhouse vehicle.

85

Evening meal for a platoon of 2nd Company *Sonderverband* 288 in early 1942, a stew with the usual ingredients of tinned Italian meat, tomatoes and reconstituted dried legumes boiling water.

Fresh bread baked by a regimental bakery company is loaded on to a truck for distribution to companies ar platoons.

FOOD AND DRINK

Peeling onions, Inf.Rgt.115 (mot) in the summer of 1941.

Kitchen area of a battery of 33rd Artillery Rgt in 15th.Pz.Div in the autumn of 1941.

The tip of a bayonet opens the Italian tin of sausage meat, the notorious 'Old Man' *(Alte Mann)* with the stamp 'AM' on the end.

Evening meal. A member of Infantry Regiment 361 in the 90th Light Division in November 1941 has constructed a stove dug into the sand with a chimney fashioned from an artillery shell that has had the detonator end cap knocked out.

A meal in the shady garden of the
O/R soldier club in Apollonia.

Water collection from a
well via hoses to fill
200-litre drums.

A Military Police (*Feldgendarmerie*) detail from 5th Light Division near Sirte in early 1941 with their Auto Union Horch cross country car (Kfz70).

German soldier shaving, using the small mirror inside his compass.

IN GENERAL

T he following photos are ones that could not be easily classified under other sections. The photos are worth reproducing, however, both for their own interest and because they are so typical. Of all the thousands of photos that passed into the hands of Allied servicemen as souvenirs, picked up at random off the battlefields, many are like these photos, with no definite background or history.

Postausgabe, Postal Delivery, somewhere in ~pt behind the Alamein e in 1942. The volume of mail handled by the *Afrikakorps* was vast.

Soldier's humour, a cactus plant with wide grin and cigarette joins the *Afrikakorps* and is given a field cap.

A not uncommon sight, letters being written before battle.

CAMOUFLAGE

Although the German High Command took little official notice of the need for the individual German soldier to camouflage himself in the desert, the men of the *Afrikakorps* did manage to blend in with their surroundings, using canvas sheets, rock mounds (sangars), piled up camelthorn, dugouts covered with equipment and battlefield debris (a most effective way of creating camouflage on the battlefield was by hiding under or among the plentiful junk left by the fighting), by painting vehicles and personal equipment with the light coloured beige or orange-tan paint supplied for vehicle camouflage and by using sand sprinkled over wet paint to completely cover reflective surfaces on metal equipment.

The faded uniforms which were so fashionable were a practical response to desert conditions, their bleached-out look made a perfect sand-coloured camouflage, making a less conspicuous contrast than the newer and darker uniforms against the light-coloured desert.

mpany Commander's
t at Alamein in 1942
decked with the usual
tufts of camelthorn.

This member of *Sonderverband* 288 wears his helmet with beige coloured paint (issued for vehicles) and a coating of sand that has been sprinkled over the still wet paint.

The vista of rocks and brush give a mottled pattern to the landscape that effectively absorbs tents covered with sprigs of camelthorn. Note the high wooden pole in the middle background, an anchor point for radio antenna. This photo was taken from high up a similar pole.

REST AND RELAXATION

T he only organised effort by the German army to entertain its troops serving out in the desert involved the *Propaganda Kompanie Afrika*, attached to *Afrikakorps* HQ, a band of wandering minstrels who sang songs, performed excerpts from popular light opera, played magical tricks on their audiences, made up bands to play modern and traditional music and showed a selection of popular movies.

Soldiers serving in the propaganda company wore grey piping on their shoulder straps and field caps, and had as their own tactical symbol a winged camel in profile, rather like a humped quadruped angel, above the letters 'PK'.

For the rest, the German soldiers in Africa made their own rest and relaxation, as the following photos show. Football games were popular, as were tug-of-war contests set up between neighbouring units. Reading and writing letters took up a lot of spare time, as did the German card game *Skat*. Food and stories involving the opposite sex helped to while away idle hours and according to Allied wartime intelligence reports, some soldiers enjoyed gambling with the little money they had. The Army's field newspaper, *Die Oase*, was well-liked and was always read from cover to cover. Radio reception was good in the desert and a fair number of European stations could be picked up on short wave radio bands from late afternoon through the early night.

An *Afrikakorps* band plays at Rommel's HQ near Gambut in the autumn of 1941 to mark the visit of Italian generals.

Any soldiers stationed in Tripoli, or passing through, were able to use the brothel operated for the German Armed Forces in the large building at 4 Via Tassoni. This brothel was serviced by Italian women.

There were facilities such as bars and canteens in Tripoli and Benghazi, and rear locations such as Derma, Tobruk, Sollum and Mersa Matruh also had places for off-duty soldiers to get a drink. These were mainly used by the transport and supply troops or quartermaster units stationed there.

A quiet and absorbing time was always in store when newspapers and journals, such as this issue of the *Berliner Illustrierter*, arrived.

Not an uncommon experience, but an attempt to ride a donkey always brought a crowd of onlookers with cameras out.

The old Roman ruins at Leptis Magna.

A visiting Italian bookshop and newsagent on wheels with German novels and writing materials.

On the beach north of Bardia, 1941. (This photo belonged to a member of M/Cycle Btln 15.)

Listening to the popular radio programmes broadcast from Germany provided occasions to gather and socialise. (15PzDiv, summer 1941.)

Italian women working in the *Wehrmacht* brothel in Tripoli.

...s were popular, such as ...s large chameleon. (Photo ...pied from a wartime book ... the *Afrikakorps.*)

Euphonium, and players, in the *Afrikakorps* band at El Alamein.

99

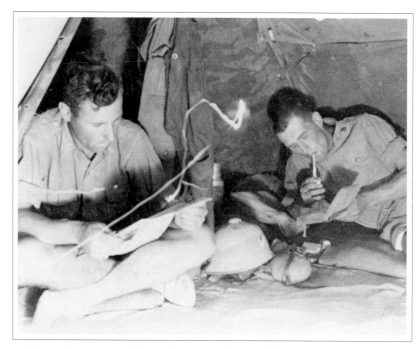

Night reading was possible inside a tent with a good lantern.

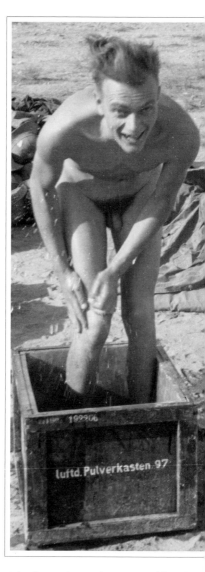

A body wash standing in metal lined ammunition cases for *Unteroffizier* Vogt Rommel's *Kampfstaffel* at Alamein in September 1942. (Dieter Hellriegel)

During the early part of 1942 a conjuror/magician attached to the *Propaganda Kompanie Afrika* toured units before Rommel's offensive against the Gazala line. Here a card miraculously appears from under a volunteer's collar.

en the top brass relaxed, as with this birthday party for General ⅃well at *Afrikakorps* HQ on 20 March, 1942.

Reading the popular DAK newspaper, *Die Oase*, which was distributed weekly through the field post system.

A game of football between teams drawn from companies stationed on the Egyptian frontier in 1941.

IN BATTLE – UNDER FIRE

Notwithstanding the difficulty of taking photos during the fighting, some troops did manage to use their cameras and the following pages show a few of their efforts (other photos snapped in battle are scattered among different parts of the book).

The phrase 'fog of war' best describes the general state of battle, where one's personal view of what was happening was clouded by an ignorance of the larger picture of things. Once battle was joined between two opposing sides a large element of the unknown was introduced. At the individual level there was a loosening of the actual control and sense of order that originated from contact with one's higher field commanders. Circumstances changed so quickly once fighting started that it was beyond communication technology alone to hold things together. Even with modern two-way radio sets in vehicles battlefield information relayed up the chain of command was often inaccurate, out of date and disjointed. Those men reporting on the battle were still limited by what they themselves saw, or perceived to be happening. The average soldier knew nothing more of the battle than what he saw by looking at the men nearest him. Friend and foe became mixed across the desert, and only the discipline and training imposed by one's own army, the morale of the soldiers themselves and their own will to win, carried the battle on.

It is therefore surprising that given the general state of battlefield chaos, with the failure of commanders to monitor effectively what was actually happening at the lowest level of organisation, most soldiers nevertheless believed *at the moment* there was still purpose and meaning and order in what was going on around them. They attributed even the smallest specific actions to intervention by some higher level of command, or as the result of some sort of prior plan. An example of this sort of belief was where an isolated random act of fire was followed by an equally indiscriminate and unconnected burst of enemy fire and in the minds of the local participants the two events were linked as to cause and effect, a sure sign that the other side was watching closely and reacting at a relatively high level of command to everything you individually, or your own side, was doing at that time. In reality the opposite was nearly always true — small units and individual soldiers were not the focus of attention by enemy commanders. It only seemed that way to the many individual soldiers scattered across the desert, immersed in the absolute importance and significance of what they themselves were doing. It was any large number of tanks together, or any columns of vehicles and guns, that seized the attention of enemy commanders. That was where threats were seen and had to be countered.

When fighting in the open and flat desert it was nearly impossible to believe you personally were not being observed by the enemy. The feeling that you were always exposed, and that the enemy knew your position, helped to give a personal meaning to the many things happening around you — an enemy plane flying overhead must be reporting on *your* position, dust thrown up in the distance by an enemy column would probably be their preliminary manoeuvres before an attack in *your* direction, artillery shells landing nearby would be aimed at *you,* and so on, regardless of whether this was true or not.

Given the lack of natural cover in the desert it was essential that commanders reacted quickly to enemy dispositions. In such conditions it becomes easier to understand how Rommel's style of command from the front was more effective, was faster to react to desert battlefield developments, than the British system of command from headquarters sited several hours away from the front lines. Rommel was able to cut through some of the 'fog of war' — until El Alamein at least — by mixing himself in the moving battle and by impressing a resolute will to win on those around him, regardless of what apparent confusion may have prevailed on the battlefield. A weaker system of command usually yielded in the belief that it must be losing if the other side held firm or attacked when it should have been retreating. Hitler firmly held this belief also, that willpower, if strong enough, could by itself turn the tide of battle in one's favour by undermining the nerve of the enemy.

Times of battle which could last over several days were invariably followed firstly by a feeling of well-being and of relief, then by a profound exhaustion that could only be overcome by sleep. This is why shots taken after the fighting had passed by often showed soldiers asleep, even in the most uncomfortable positions.

After the fierce fighting around Bir Hacheim in June 1942 a member of 2nd Company of *Sonderverband* 288 sleeps exhausted in a trench.

Battle was not continuous, it ebbed and flowed like the tides, and there were times of apparent calm when meals could be eaten, weapons and equipment checked, bowels emptied, and petrol, ammunition, water, food and other supplies brought up by the transport columns. Photos show it was common at such times for soldiers to get out bundles of letters from their packs and read them.

What one did in battle was largely determined by one's training, by a conditioned response to obey orders, and by the cohesiveness of the basic fighting unit. There was little imaginative or creative thinking involved in handling weapons. The first time under enemy fire was terrifying and unnerving, and it was always like this. With time each soldier found his own way of accepting the strain of battle, and of living with its brutality. The comradeship of the close-knit combat units made it somewhat easier to face up to what became an intimate shared experience. For those who faced enemy fire alone, especially those cut off from their comrades and under fire, it was far, far worse. For these soldiers, all alone, the psychological strains were enormous, and unrelenting, with thoughts of death or maiming injury never far away.

During the fighting south of Gazala in May 1942 two infantry seek some rest and shade under canvas shelter quarters buttoned together and slung from wooden stakes. Behind them is their foxhole with rifles propped up on the edge.

A blurry shot of a 10.5-cm howitzer with muzzle depressed firing at an approaching enemy column November 1941.

An artillery crew snapped during a meal pause in the desert south of Mersa Matruh in late June 1942 as the DAK surrounded British forces there blocking the way along the coastal road.

eneral Grant tanks knocked out after they had come against a line of
3-mm guns in the early stages of the Gazala battle in May/June 1942.

by Allied bombers. (NZ soldier's photo)

General von Bismarck, commander of the 21st Panzer Division (in glasses and peaked cap) snapped during the fighting before the capture of Tobruk in 1942.

The aftermath of battle, bodies and personal possessions lying scattered on the desert where artillery or mortar fire had caught them without protection. (British dead at El Alamein.)

Two photos taken by Paul-Erich Schäfler in June 1941 from the position his battery of 15.5-cm guns held on the Egyptian border.

Training, March 1942, an officer running forward with his men has his drawn pistol in his hand. (In reality, these light and short range hand weapons were almost never used.)

After the capture of Bir Hacheim, these members of 2nd Company *Sonderverband* 288 sit together with food and drink

Mortar firing during the bitter
fighting for Bir Hacheim in June
1942; here the real thing, from
2nd Company *Sonderverband*
288.

Tank crewman's view, dust from
an enemy artillery shell hangs in
the air as a following tank skirts
the point of impact.

The popular image: in foxhole
with gun at ready.

111

Watching fall of shot through scissor periscope binoculars while two men in the rear hold telephones to their ears waiting to relay information back to the gun batteries.

A 17-cm Kanone 18 of *Sonderverband* 288 moving up into battle in June 1942 (note the white air recognition band across the bonnet of the prime mover).

ARTILLERY

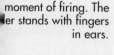

Red was the distinguishing colour worn on caps and shoulder straps by artillery regiments (the same colour edging to the shoulder straps as shown by general rank officers). The artillery regiments serving in the Panzer Divisions in Africa had an establishment strength of approximately 2,000 (the artillery regiments in Infantry and Light Divisions were slightly smaller in size), though these full establishment figures were hardly ever reached in reality.

The artillery batteries, the basic tactical units, were closely integrated into the combat chain of command, responding even to requests for supporting fire from unit commanders as low as platoon leaders who could ask for fire against specified targets in their immediate area. Artillery fire was responsible for the greatest number of casualties on both sides in the North African campaigns. The stony ground absorbed very little of the force of exploding shells, with most of the lethal shrapnel therefore flying outwards to strike down anyone in range. Shrapnel from airburst fire was also a major cause of battlefield casualties.

moment of firing. The
ler stands with fingers
in ears.

Whenever the *Luftwaffe* lost air supremacy, artillery sites were particularly vulnerable to enemy strafing by the hated and feared Fighter-bombers, the *Jabos*. The artillery guns were also likely to receive counter-battery fire from the enemy's artillery. Artillery displacements therefore were given some protection by putting up rings of rocks and sandbags whenever there was time to build these protective walls. These defensive walls did not completely enclose the gun sites; there always had to be at least one open side for the tractors to pull the guns away quickly, an important factor in such a mobile war. The tents used by the soldiers were always pitched some way away from where the guns were dug in.

However, all too often in battle the artillery batteries did not have time to protect themselves with stoneworks and by digging in, and they suffered from being exposed to enemy counter fire. Because of the clouds of dust thrown up by artillery guns when they fired, it was impossible to conceal their location once firing had started.

As with all other weapons, the fine desert dust was a constant problem for artillery gunners. Shells had to be carefully brushed to remove grains of sand, even when the shells were taken from stores and still packed in their wicker baskets. It was heavy work manhandling shells; their great weight meant crews had to work very hard while their guns were in action. Manhandling the guns themselves also called for great physical effort on the part of their crews.

Artillery units suffered heavy losses, especially when overrun after standing to fight off an enemy advancing with tanks. The heavier guns of the artillery batteries meant these units were nowhere near as mobile as the lighter anti-tank guns. The exception to this was of course when the artillery guns were mounted on a tank chassis as an 'Assault Gun', though such weapons were only seen in any number in Tunisia. Unlike their *Luftwaffe* counterparts manning anti-aircraft guns, army artillery crews initially were not issued with steel helmets in North Africa.

10.5 cm *leichte Feldhaubi[t]* 18 (light field howitzer) wi[th] its Krauss-Maffei half-track prime mover in 1942, aro[und] the time of the capture of Tobruk.

Captured French heavy artillery piece, the 15.5-cm *Canon de 155 GPF-T (Grand Puissance Filloux-Touzard)* in Western Cyrenaica in early 1942.

General view of war from the artillery gunner's position, moving up to and away from the gun as it is loaded and fired again and again . . .

ach artillery unit had its own signals platoon, and guns were always linked by ephone cables to OP sites, with their distinctive 'scissor' binocular periscopes up behind rocky parapets. From these OP sites it was possible to register the ual fall of shot and to communicate this information directly to the battery of ns. It was standard practice for artillery batteries to have three observation sts, one sited near the guns, another as close as possible to the front, and the d being integrated into the main line of resistance (i.e. behind the actual front in the fallback position).

Ammunition supplies were a continuing problem because of the critical overall pply situation, and because of the large number of various 'booty' guns used the *Afrikakorps* (British, French, Russian etc.) requiring their own special pply of ammunition.

Heinz Köllenberger of 33rd Artl. Rgt in 15 Panzer Division with a captured British 87.6-cm 25-pounder on the Egyptian border, July 1941.

Moving a captured British 5.5-in howitzer used by 164th Light Div. at El Alamein into position in soft sand took an enormous physical effort, even with such large wheels.

ARTILLERY

A series of shots taken of a battery of the standard German army field howitzer of World War II, the 15-cm *schwere Feldhaubitze* 18, here in position north-west of Sidi Omar in late 1941.

Shells in wicker baskets stacked in readiness behind, and empty propellant cases lined up ready for use in charging the shells once they had been rammed into the breach.

Priming the detonator in the nose cone of the shell.

Side view of the battery showing all four guns.

After the action, the barrel is depressed to lower the silhouette and a light camouflage net has been thrown across the whole gun.

'Braut des Infanteristen' (Bride of the Infantry), the bolt action Mauser rifle model Kar98k used by the majority of soldiers in the *Afrikakorps*. This expression, used quite affectionately by German soldiers in World War II, had its origins in the First World War, where it had been also widely used with the Mod98 Mauser rifle.

Infantry commander, Hans-Günter Baade (centre), in early 1942 the commander of the 115th Rifle (Motorised Infantry) Regiment in 15th Panzer Division.

INFANTRY, AFRICAN GRENADIERS

...oon after firing a rifle ...to be cleaned. It was ...ourt martial offence to have a dirty weapon.

T he motorised infantry units in the *Afrikakorps* in 1941, and for most of 1942, were known as Rifle Regiments *(Schützenregimenter),* but from the second half of 1942 were renamed Panzer Grenadier Regiments *(Panzergrenadier-regimenter).* There were no infantry units at all in the first division despatched to Africa, the 5th Light Div., and its two MG battalions and engineer troops had to take on the role of infantry. The divisions that followed later had their full share of motorised infantry regiments. Few infantry soldiers in Africa wore steel helmets until the fighting in Tunisia when they were in general issue.

The various motorised infantry units wore green piping on caps and shoulder straps, this colour being the most commonly seen among the combat units, reflecting their large numerical strength in the divisions during 1941 and 1942. In Tunisia there was one division with a regiment of unmotorised infantry, the 334th Division, and these 'foot' soldiers wore white piping on their shoulder straps (the other 'infantry' regiment in this division contained alpine troops and they wore a medium green colour).

When a line had to be held, it was not done with minefields and artillery alone or the anti-tank guns. Along the miles of 'front' were the infantry and their weapons which they had to carry themselves — mortars, machine guns, machine pistols, rifles and grenades. Theirs was the job of actually occupying the edge of whatever piece of territory happened to be in dispute.

Although the *Afrikakorps* was a fully motorised force, the need to fight from static positions meant that the motorised infantry very quickly became ordinary infantry 'foot' soldiers fighting from trenches and foxholes. After twelve days of heavy fighting at El Alamein in October and November 1942, the *Afrikakorps* had lost a high proportion of its Panzer Grenadier strength, and these losses (along with the all important Panzers) made it impossible for Rommel to hold on any longer. Although in numbers alone Rommel still commanded a large force, with the front line infantry units down to very low numbers, the British offensive could not be held and their relentless advance quickened, causing Rommel to order the retreat, even before Berlin and Hitler had been informed.

Along with mental pictures of the dusty Panzers and their crews, it is the image of an infantry soldier in bleached cloth field cap with rifle in hand in a foxhole that fills the popular image of the *Afrikakorps*. And rightly so.

The deadly MG42, the machine gun that had a phenomenal 1400 rpm max. rate of fire, first used in Africa by the German army in May 1942, had a sound like no other gun used by either side.

The typical face of the German infantry soldier in Africa, in faded field cap, overcoat in the early morning and late afternoon, with Kar98k slung over one shoulder, and dotted with flies.

At least one unit did not throw away their gas masks in the desert. These soldiers have just had an exercise using their gas masks, late 1941. (The gas masks here are worn around the neck on canvas straps.)

During a lull in the fighting near the Gazala cauldron in June 1942, men from MG Battalion 8 with their 'booty' British lorry.

Training in the early part of 1942, members of 2nd Company of *Sonderverband* 288 firing an MG34 from a trench protected by a line of sandbags.

El Alamein: two soldiers loaded with the paraphernalia of infantry — machine pistol, steel helmet, water bottles, ammunition, bread bag, mess tins. The man on the right carries the heavy weight of a base plate for a mortar on his back.

Wheels of war, members of 2nd Company *Sonderverband* 288 with their personal equipment piled up on their 2.8-cm anti-tank weapon, a *Panzerbüsche* 41 with tapering bore-barrel which fired a tungsten-tipped projectile. The soldier to the left holds a British souvenir cap.

The highly successful close range infantry weapon, the automatic MP40 Machine Pistol.

A captured British 40-mm Bofors AA gun taken over by members of the 2nd Company in Sonderverband 288. Captured weapons and transport were often of crucial importance to the outcome of a battle.

(Above and left): By the end of 1942 Rommel was pulling the survivors of his *Afrikakorps* back across the Gulf of Sirte into Tripolitania. Here a mortar crew train their weapon (an 8-cm *Granatenwerfer* 34) towards the east, towards the British lines. Open boxes of mortar bombs are arranged near the entrance to their covered-over earth bunker.(Charles Hinz)

CHAPTER 16

A wounded Grenadier from 90th Light Division picked up on the battlefield on 2 November, 1942. His right hand shows signs of advanced gangrene resulting from a tightly applied ligature.

Lining up for a cholera booster at a medical dressing station in 1941.

MEDICAL

Medical units were organised firstly inside each division, at company level for field hospitals, dressing stations, ambulance sections, and stores and supplies. The second level of medical support services, in the larger hospitals sited in the rear (in Tripoli and Benghazi for 1941), usually came under direct corps or army administration. These large base hospitals were fully equipped with surgical theatres, X-Ray plant, plaster cast and resuscitation sections as well as the critical care wards. These hospitals, especially the ones at Tripoli and Derna, were most used in 1941 and early 1942, Later in 1942, when the *Afrikakorps* found itself deep inside Egyptian territory, it was easier to transport wounded by air from airfields in Egypt to the large Wehrmacht hospitals in Athens. Such a trip was in fact shorter than going back to Tripoli and hospitals in Greece or Italy did not have to be supplied with materials and staff carried across the Mediterranean.

Personnel serving in medical units wore a dark blue piping on their field caps and shoulder straps. Medical units were made up of very high numbers of volunteers, including those who had offered themselves for this non-combatant role, such as those for whom religious beliefs precluded actual fighting. Female nurses also served in the field hospitals in Africa, with exceptional bravery and devotion to their patients. In all, about two hundred female nurses went to Africa with the *Afrikakorps* and served alongside their male colleagues.

The German army's attitude to treating their wounded was really quite simple: they aimed to identify as quickly as possible those who could be returned to their units after treatment, and to ensure that those with serious injuries received appropriate medical care with maximum speed.

In the open desert the forward hospitals or dressing stations were no more than a collection of large tents, one of which served as a mortuary. In times of fighting the mortuary would always contain bodies awaiting burial, many only half-dressed and still showing the evidence of recent surgery as well as their wounds. In order to get a seriously wounded man to the operating table as quickly as possible, only the clothing in the immediate vicinity of the wound(s) would be removed, cut away with long handled shears. If these men died during surgery, they were carried to the mortuary tent and left as they had come off the operating table. In the middle of battle there was no time to lay out the bodies as one would in a funeral parlour.

Anyone who spent time serving in one of these forward field hospitals, and the smaller dressing or medical aid stations, never forgot the odour that was associated with those places — a mixture of blood, perspiration, ether and antiseptic solution. These forward dressing stations received their patients on stretchers delivered by ambulances or by truck. They dressed all wounds, and could handle blood transfusions, the administration of drugs, splinting of fractures, and most types of emergency surgery including amputations. As much as possible the forward dressing stations attempted to save lives by stabilising the condition of the more seriously wounded who would get specialised treatment later at the larger hospitals to the rear. This was the case for serious chest and abdominal wounds, and skull damage. Those seriously wounded were evacuated quickly by air from the combat zone if it was possible, firstly by small Feiseler Storks to one of the larger base hospitals, and then back to Europe. In 1941 and 1942 this meant travelling by hospital ship to Naples, or by air to Athens. Evacuation of wounded from Tunisia was efficiently organised using fleets of Ju52s flying from the many former French airfields, right up to the last hours of the campaign. For most of those sick or wounded who were evacuated to Europe a long period of recovery was ahead of them, for some stretching into many months.

The greatest single cause of wounds, and death, for soldiers in Africa was from artillery fire. Other main causes of battlefield casualties were aerial strafing and bombing, from mines, and MG fire (usually fired over some distance). Apart from critical damage to one of the vital organs which resulted in almost instant death, most battlefield deaths came from loss of blood, shock, and dehydration. It says a lot for the standard of care in the forward dressing stations that there were not many deaths attributable to infected wounds.

At El Alamein the living conditions were so unhygienic that in August and September 1942 more men were being withdrawn from their units and repatriated to Europe because of sickness than from battle-related wounds. Indeed, for a period in August and September 1942 the number of sick being repatriated exceeded the number of new replacements reaching the front line units. Serious bowel disorders were particularly common, usually necessitating hospitalisation in Europe. Skin ulcers that constantly discharged were a problem too, though not in the same category as the bowel diseases. Jaundice was another common condition that ultimately required treatment in Europe if the patient was to recover. Even so, in these difficult conditions the average German managed to keep himself relatively clean, German military discipline saw to this. Axis medical records showed that for every one German infested by lice there were on average ten Italians who urgently needed delousing.

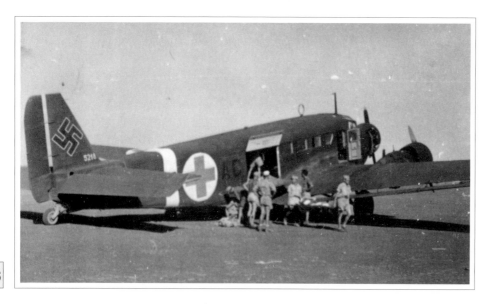

A Ju52 painted with a red cross unloads its cargo of wounded *Afrikakorps* soldie at a Greek airfield outside Athens.

An Italian hospital ship anchored in Bardia Harbour in September 1941. Such ships were the main means of evacuating wounded troops back to Europe in 1941 and for the first half of 1942.

A wounded member of 2nd Company *Sonderverband* 288 stands supported by two comrades in front of an Italian ambulance in June 1942.

Booster shots against Paratyphoid or Cholera in the early part of 1942. The injections were given into the chest muscle rather than into the arm which may have rendered the arm useless for a time with any severe reaction against the immunising dose (left side of chest for those right handed, right side chest for left handed).

A cigarette while lying waiting on a stretcher for the next stage of the evacuation back to the base hospital at Derna in May 1942.

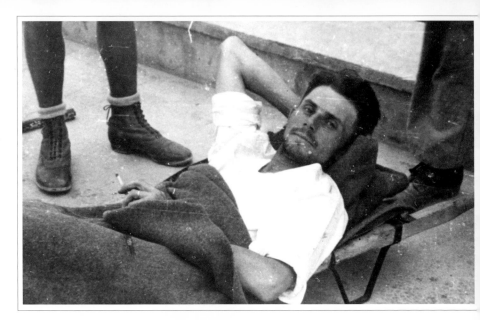

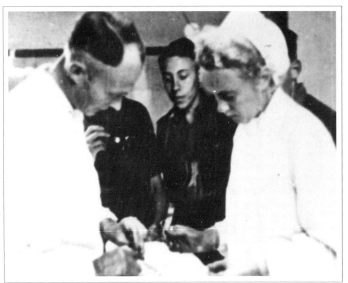

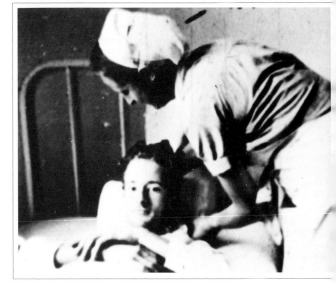

Two shots taken in the summer of 1941 in Tripoli of nurses and patients in the hospital operated by Field Hospital 200 which was attached to the 5th Light Division (later 21st Panzer Division).

The Forward Dressing Station of 21st Panzer Division situated west of Bardia in November 1941.

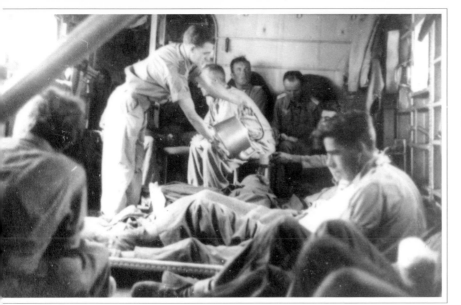

Interior of a bus that had been converted into an ambulance.

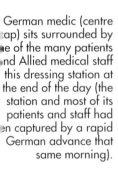

German medic (centre cap) sits surrounded by some of the many patients and Allied medical staff at this dressing station at the end of the day (the station and most of its patients and staff had been captured by a rapid German advance that same morning).

During the fighting around the Tobruk perimeter in November 1941, this tank was used to bring up urgently needed medical supplies.

CHAPTER 17

Cross-country acclimatisation trips, navigating by sun and compass.

April 1941. Fresh arrivals in Libya, with motorcycles and uniforms not yet showing signs of desert wear.

MOTORCYCLE BATTALION

T he one Motorcycle Battalion in *Afrikakorps,* the famous 15th Battalion under *Oberstleutnant* Knabe (its first commander) came to Libya with the 15th Panzer Division. The battalion took part in nearly all of the major battles in the North African campaign. Its primary function was one of fast battlefield reconnaissance, though it was also used as motorised infantry by Rommel in the first half of 1941. The battalion lost its separate identity after the end of 1941 when it was absorbed as a third battalion by Rifle Rgt 115 in 15 PzDiv. In spite of the battalion officially changing its name, such was the force and strength of its identity as '15th Motorcycle Battalion' that it continued to be known by its old title for a long time, even when its activities were being officially recorded in the war diary of the *Panzergruppe Afrika* in 1942.

While the primary function of the battalion may have been to carry out quick battlefield reconnaissance and to filter through any gaps in the enemy's line, not all vehicles used by the battalion were motorcycles. In its make-up the battalion also had its allocation of half tracks, anti-tank guns, signals vehicles and its own transport lorries.

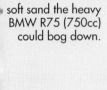

soft sand the heavy BMW R75 (750cc) could bog down.

131

CHAPTER 17

The 15th Motorcycle Battalion, as the major component in Battlegroup Geissler, suffered terrible losses in an engagement with the 28th (Maori) NZ Battalion supported by the NZ Divisional Cavalry Regiment on 3 December 1941. The casualties were so severe that the battalion was nearly wiped out. Travelling down the Via Balbia towards Bardia it was ambushed by the New Zealanders who had spotted its advance and were lying in wait. The only support for the motorcycles pinned down under withering fire by the New Zealanders came from a solitary long range artillery piece firing indiscriminately from inside Bardia. The 15th Motorcycle Battalion bravely counter-attacked but could not make any advance against the stronger NZ positions. By the end of the day only forty-eight Germans, officers, NCOs and ORs got away out of a strength of around 450 that morning. Among the prisoners taken that day was the battalion commander, Major von Debschitz. After this disastrous engagement Rommel had to order that the survivors of the battalion were not to be used in front line combat until further notice. The battalion was rebuilt in early 1942 and fought again and again with distinction in the campaigns throughout 1942, and into 1943.

In 1941 troops serving in the Motorcycle Battalion wore a special soft shade of green piping on their shoulder straps and caps but this was replaced by copper brown in late 1941 (the same colour being used by reconnaissance units).

Changing a sidecar wheel

Maintenance, with a supporting jerrican beneath the sump.

MOTORCYCLE BATTALION

About to slip another tube over a wheel rim.

Holes in the mudguard show where the edge of a burst of enemy MG fire has arced past.

November 1941. Nights were getting cold and the long coat was good protection against the cold air until the sun was up.

The owner of the camera that took most of the photos in this section, in the late part of 1941.

A lorry belonging to Anti-tank Unit 39, the very first part of the Afrikakorps to arrive in Libya, with three men of this unit, soon after reaching the front in late February 1941.

Driver of the lorry in the photo above after the vehic had been given its desert camouflage in a light sand yellow paint very early in th campaign, around mid-March 1941.

PAK AND FLAK

T ogether with the tank crews, the PAK (anti-tank) units were the hard hitting edge of the *Afrikakorps,* both shield to the spear of the Panzer regiments, and anvil to their hammer.

It was fitting that the PAK crews wore the same pink piping on their caps and shoulder straps as the tank regiments. The anti-tank guns, and their gunners, were just as much a part of the tank battles as were the crews of the tanks. The long-barrelled anti-tank guns themselves were found not just in the specialist PAK units. They were used by reconnaissance, engineer, armoured infantry, and even HQ staff sections as main line protection against enemy tanks.

The anti-tank gunners wore steel helmets, unlike the gunners manning the heavier artillery, who were usually further behind the front line (as long as the fighting was not moving from place to place around the desert).

Half tracked prime movers with the distinctive long-barrelled PAK guns towed behind were never far from the Panzers in battle, and in retreat it was always the PAK guns that were among the last to pull back as the enemy advanced.

In fast moving battles of 1941 and the first half of 1942, anti-tank gunners fought in the open with no cover other than the small shields mounted on the guns, or what was given by the half track vehicles they travelled in. The PAK units usually moved right up with the tanks, and when the tanks stopped then so must their anti-tank escort, wherever it might be and usually without the time to dig in before fighting resumed.

ical configuration, the
n PAK 38 with its light
-tracked prime mover
Kfz.10) carrying crew
and ammunition.

Changing position without the horsepower of the prime mover takes the united effort of the seven-man crew of this 5 cm PAK 38 (*Sonderverband* 288, May 1942).

The rare 4.2 cm lePAK 41, a tapered bore weapon firing special tungsten core ammunition, here as used by *Sonderverband* 288 in early 1942.

After the Alamein retreat *Sonderverband* 288 formed the rearguard for Rommel's retreat back the Gulf of Sirte. Here two crew of a 5-cm PAK wait in their prepared position near Mersa Matruh, November 1942. (Out of sight their tractor stands ready to move the gun and its crew at short notice.)

The original German anti-tank gun with a tapered barrel to fire special tungsten core ammunition, the 2.8 cm sPZB41, which narrowed to 2 cm at the barrel exit point. This example from 2nd Company of *Sonderverband* 288 in early 1942.

Crew positions for the 4.2 cm lePAK 41 (light anti-tank gun model 41).

British Matilda 'I' tank, stopped
by German PAK fire near Halfaya
in July 1941.

Left in the retreat from El Alamein, when it could
not longer fight on, this 88 crew 'spiked' their gun
by blocking the barrel and firing a round. This gun
must have been firing during the retreat; it is not
dug in and has only a few sandbags and rocks as
protection, sure signs the crew had not been in that
position for very long (Australian solider's photo).

Mainstay of the DAK
anti-tank units in 1941, the
5 cm PAK 38, here in an
ordnance repair base.

Flak units were drawn from both the army and the *Luftwaffe*. (Army anti-aircraft units were designated 'Fla.' to distinguish them from the *Luftwaffe* units who took the more commonly used 'Flak'.) For both services, it was ground action rather than anti-aircraft fire that provided the bulk of their action in the desert. The single most powerful weapon used on the North African battlefield was an anti-aircraft gun that was the supreme battlefield anti-tank weapon, the high-velocity 88-mm capable of firing against tanks with the accuracy of a sniper's rifle. There was no Allied tank in North Africa able to withstand the 88-mm guns. Nearly all of the 88-mm gunners were *Luftwaffe* personnel, but they fulfilled the role of anti-tank gunners like their army counterparts. The *Luftwaffe* saw to it that their Flak soldiers all had steel helmets.

The smaller automatic cannons originally designed for low altitude anti-aircraft fire were also employed in front line fighting against ground targets by their army and *Luftwaffe* crews. Against lightly armed vehicles and 'soft-skinned' transport lorries such weapons were highly destructive.

Army anti-aircraft units wore white piping on their caps and shoulder straps, and the *Luftwaffe* Flak units wore red.

ur views of Army Flak
ttalion 606 loading
nicles and guns at Naples
23 March 1941.

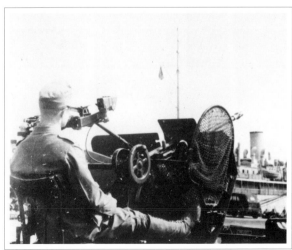

Motorcycles were an important part of the panzer regiments. This one from 15 PzDiv (1st Company PzRgt 8) is loading in Naples, April 1941.

PANZERS

T hough in popular imagination they epitomise the *Afrikakorps*, in numbers the panzer crews were only a fraction of the total strength in the German divisions of the *Afrikakorps*. In the Panzer divisions themselves, the number of officers and soldiers in a Panzer regiment did not number more than 1,800 (including Rgt HQ staff, signals platoon, workshop company and supply column) out of a total theoretical divisional strength of 12,500. Pink piping on caps and shoulder straps, and the distinctive metal skull badges affixed to tunic lapels, marked their uniforms apart as belonging to a panzer crew. They used the small metal skulls removed from the lapel badges on their black woollen Continental uniforms, and attached the skulls to the lapels of their tropical tunics. This simple modification to their uniform insignia set the tank crews apart from any other arm of the service in the *Afrikakorps* (even within their own arm of service, the pink piping was worn by everyone in the regiment, even company paymasters and cooks wore it). The panzer crews were an élite, they knew it, and they showed it with their collar skull badges.

Just as important as the tank crews inside their 'steel coffins' were the recovery and maintenance crews who worked on and off the battlefield to restore damaged tanks back to fighting condition. Another essential service supporting the tanks was provided by the transport and supply units who had to bring the ammunition and petrol right up to the tanks on the battlefield. These support services were an integral part of the panzer regiments.

Death rates in the Panzer regiments were high, indicating not only the scale of action involving these men but the high risks they faced in their 'steel coffins'.

Panzer Regiment 8, on the Egyptian frontier in May 1941, make a halt for a meal with a small car from Recc. Unit 3 point 206 (inland from Bardia).

Hammock strung alongside a PzI of the regimental HQ company.

Basic maintenance was carried out by the tanks' own crews; weapons maintenance such as cleaning and greasing, replacing the road wheels, and adjusting the tension of the tracks, as this crew of a PzII from 15th PzDiv are doing in the autumn of 1941.

PzIII moving at speed through desert dust, the dust that clogged air filters and penetrated every moving part of the machine, accelerating wear and tear, especially on tracks and wheels.

PzIII in a repair workshop during the fighting of late 1941.

Tank crew photo after the award of the silver Tank Assault badge in July 1941. (Paul Kenwary)

143

The stencilled signs on the armour of this PzIII show the palm tree and swastika tactical symbol of the *Afrikakorps* and the two quadrants symbol of the 21st Pz Division. (Paul Warnsbrough)

Two of several photos taken in the workshops established to the west of Tobruk in 1941.
Above: Dropping the repaired engine back into a PzIII.
Right: A lathe worker in machine workshop.

Alamein, and the face
of a seasoned desert
Panzer gunner.

...apped by a member of
PzReg 8 during the
...ting near Sidi Rezegh,
...late November 1941.

145

Front view of a PzIII in early 1942. The spare track draped across the hull of the tank acted as an extra layer of protective armour.

A PzIII snapped during the fighting in late 1941.

PzIII, PzRgt8, front view, early summer 1941.

A PzIII that had the misfortune to drive over a mine during the Sollum Battle of June 1941.

Tripoli, March 1941, and Italian women lining the road throw flowers at Panzers of PzRgt5 driving off to the east.

Battle, PzIII and its victim, Libya, December 1941.

147

37 mm anti-tank gun of a *Pionier* HQ staff company.

On the Egyptian border in the summer of 1941, three of these sapper soldiers are wearing their gauze mesh mosquito/fly protective head nets. The half track vehicle is a Sd.Kfz 250/2 and the stone cairn at left conceals a periscope binocular.

PIONEERS

The Pioneers or *Pioniere* were the combat engineers, the sappers, the ones who went in first during an attack, the ones who lifted the enemy mines, cut a path through the barbed wire for others to follow, and who placed the explosive charges next to the enemy bunkers. They were the storm troops of the Panzer divisions in the *Afrikakorps*. These units, organised as an *Abteilung* or light battalion were assigned to each division. These élite assault troops wore black piping on their caps and shoulder straps.

It was they who had to accept hand-to-hand fighting, 'Close Combat', using grenades and machine pistols as well as bayonets and entrenching tools. This sort of fighting, so often described in war stories, rarely happened in fact. When it did, it was very likely the *Pioniere* who had to do it, the same pioneers who were usually the first to advance and the last to retreat, laying mines and booby traps as they went.

A medium signals car *(rch)* Kfz15 of the Staff Company of a *Pionier Abteilung* at Fort Capuzzo in 1941. (The insignia faintly visible on the left front mudguard makes this entification possible, a tangle with wheels on lower corners and a ed arrow on the top.)

The now familiar dockside architecture of Naples harbour frames vehicles and equipment of Reconnaissance Unit 3 in February 1941.

An observation post manned by men from Recc. Unit 33 (15PzDiv) in 1941 on the edge of the escarpment above Halfaya displays a 'No Parking' sign and a machine gun mounted on an AA tripod.

A half track prime mover (Sd.Kfz.10) of Recc. Unit 3 with attached supplies trailer on a Mediterranean beach in early May 1941.

RECONNAISSANCE

When the desert campaigns started, the reconnaissance units (*Aufklärungs Abteilungen*, abbreviated to AA) still wore the traditional cavalry colour of gold yellow as the piping on their shoulder straps and field caps. By the end of 1941 they had been given a new identifying colour, copper brown, to distinguish them from cavalry units. The importance of reconnaissance can be gauged by the strength of these *Abteilungen* in the Panzer divisions, over 800 men, consisting of an HQ staff with a signals platoon, two armoured car companies, a motorcycle company, a heavy weapons company (anti-tank and artillery) and their own supply column. In Africa it was common to see this considerable strength reinforced with even more PAK and Flak weapons, often mounted on flat top lorries or half track vehicles, to create a stronger hitting force better able to break quickly through enemy lines.

The main function of the reconnaissance units was to accelerate an advance against enemy territory. Quick and deep penetration was vital to the success of new tactics designed for modern, mobile armoured warfare. These units were used aggressively, not only to obtain up to the minute battlefield information but actually to take possession of the territory being reconnoitred. In every campaign fought in Africa, the reconnaissance units featured prominently.

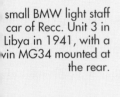

small BMW light staff car of Recc. Unit 3 in Libya in 1941, with a ...vin MG34 mounted at the rear.

Telephone switchboard inside a communications van attached to a regimental HQ is home to a chameleon.

Radio base, here set up next to an eight-wheel armoured car from a Signals *Abteilung* in the late summer of 1941.

Rigging telephone cables in 1941 outside Tobruk. The vehicle in the background is a Büssing NAG survey party truck, Kfz 415.

Typical signals point, radio car with aerials strung up on poles.

SIGNALS

The identifying colour worn on the uniforms of these units was a pale lemon yellow. Radio and telephone lines were the main means of relaying information on and off the battlefield. The signals units were fully motorised and highly mobile, with their own special armoured vehicles packed with radio transmitters and receivers. Normally, the companies of the *Nachrichten Abteilung*, or signals detachment, were dispersed throughout the division according to the need parts of the division had to maintain contact with each other. The usual strength of a signals *Abteilung* was around 400.

When the fighting was localised and carried on from stationary positions greater use was made of telephones because they were a more secure medium for passing messages, even without codes. The first units to lay their own telephone cables after stopping anywhere were the various level HQ staffs, followed by artillery batteries and then those units closest to the enemy who needed to report their observations to higher levels of command. Some signals equipment, usually the telephone, was also operated by personnel not serving in signals units. Such telephone systems were operated by regular members of other units who had done special signals training rather than by members drawn from the signals units themselves.

company commander rides in a special half-ck vehicle fitted with a tubular frame radio aerial.

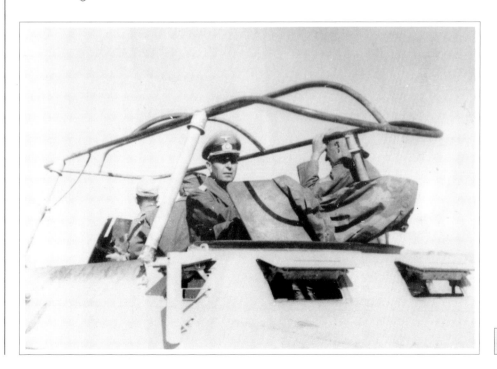

Spaced out to minimise the risk of being hit by enemy aircraft, the columns of supply vehicles follow the direction of the front line.

Men in a transport unit celebrating the award of decorations in early 1943. The awards are the Italo-German African Commerative Medal (pinned under pocket flap) and the War Service Cross with Swords (with ribbon attached to buttonhole).

TRANSPORT AND SUPPLY

T roops serving in these units wore sky blue piping on their field caps and shoulder straps. The soldiers whose job it was to drive supply trucks in Africa covered enormous distances, as was shown by a special award given to those drivers who had performed outstanding service, many of whom had driven over 100,000 km. Their primary task was to ensure the supply of ammunition, fuel and rations to the front line units, and the movement to the rear again of unused ammunition and whatever could be picked up from the battlefield and recycled.

Each division had its own transport and supply columns, responsible for ferrying material between the various storage points or depots and the front. The rear zone supply units who also ferried supplies and who looked after the rear material dumps came under overall command of the corps or army quartermasters.

Members of these units attached to major fighting formations should not be considered as rear support troops. Supplies carried from corps and divisional dumps (or 'parks' as the Germans called them) in the rear had to be taken right up to the front line by these drivers, and they regularly came under fire on the battlefield from enemy guns and tanks. They suffered particularly heavy losses from strafing and bombing attacks by the Allied air forces. In those periods when battle was joined by the two sides, the transport columns were often caught in the cross-fire.

It does not need to be pointed out that without supplies an army cannot survive, and in Africa absolutely everything had to be transported to the front, even drinking water and wood to fire the German army's mobile kitchen.

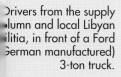

Drivers from the supply column and local Libyan militia, in front of a Ford (German manufactured) 3-ton truck.

A small tracked vehicle used to pull away heavy material landed on the beach by flat-bottom vessels in Bardia during the late summer of 1942.

Wooden crates containing food were stacked in squares three crates high and then covered with camelthorn brush as camouflage.

Among the shallow draft vessels used to bring supplies into Bardia in 1942 were these two – a fishing scow and a barge that has had the words 'HAMBURG' and 'DAK' painted across the bow.

vs of jerricans cover the water's edge at Bardia in the late summer
942. These jerricans full of gasoline, probably landed from a
marine, are swollen by the heat of the noon-day sun

Transport column with its NCO leader's
Volkswagen being pushed up a slope
slippery with loose rubble.

The heavy traffic along the
defined tracks through the
desert turned them into
highways of powdery dust up
to 60 cm deep.

CHAPTER 24

A very typical burial performed at or near the site of death, a shallow grave covered in rocks with simple grave markers, here bearing the legend 'Two unknown German Soldiers, Fallen on 16 June 1941'. Two broken parts of German rifles and a pith helmet complete the visible marking of this grave site.

The German-Italian cemetery just outside Bardia in the summer of 1941. (The star represented the Italian Royal House of Savoy.)

The battlefield grave of *Gefreiter* Xaver Andrelang of 2nd Company *Sonderverband* 288, killed in May 1942.

| # GRAVES

G raves were one of the subjects most photographed by German soldiers in North Africa, taken both to make a personal record of where comrades were buried in an otherwise featureless desert, and to have prints to send back to families of dead comrades in Germany.

Unit after unit in 1941 took photos of three main Libyan burial grounds — at Km41 (to the west of Tobruk); just south of Bardia (both of these contained German and Italian dead); and the German cemetery in front of the damaged Fort Capuzzo. By 1942 the number of such official cemeteries had grown enormously. As well as the already established military cemeteries, it was quite common to find single graves, or two or three, near a burnt out tank or vehicle, marked by a simple wooden cross or stake. Quite often only some parts of a body could be found for burial, the missing pieces having been fragmented in an explosion, or burnt, and lost. In December 1942 a company commander in 15th Panzer Division, standing in conversation with other officers had his head blown away from his torso by a direct hit from a high velocity anti-tank shell, most likely solid shot which did not detonate on impact. His comrades searched the desert in vain . . .

All wartime grave sites were temporary, from the smallest to the largest. By the time of the final retreat from El Alamein in November 1942, there were already over four thousand German dead killed in Egypt, buried in the various cemeteries stretching from areas behind the Alamein position itself and from Sidi Abd el Rahman and El Daba back to Mersa Matruh. These cemeteries, and the large number of grave sites in Libya, survived into the immediate post-war years.

The isolated single graves on the battlefield, however, were shifted for reburial in the many larger cemeteries nearer the coast as soon as possible in the months after the fighting by the Allied Graves Registration Companies. Only after the war were all bodies disinterred from the larger wartime graveyards and collected during the 1950s for reburial in the three permanent German cemeteries in North Africa. El Alamein (Egypt), Tobruk (Libya), and Bordj Cedria (Tunisia). Today there are 4,549 buried in the El Alamein cemetery, 6,026 in the Tobruk cemetery and just over 8,000 in Bordj Cedria.

Wartime battlefield German graves often had a steel helmet or pith helmet left on top as markers, but such objects did not long survive to passing souvenir-hunting Allied armies. In rocky ground, graves had to be shallow for it was difficult to excavate a deep enough space in the hard ground. This gave graves the appearance of mounds, which is essentially what they were, built up above ground to enclose the corpse.

In many cases burial was an act performed by one's enemy. That it was usually done with some fair measure of decency and respect says a lot about the regard the ordinary soldiers of the opposing armies in the desert had for each other.

A German cemetery near Tunis in 1943. In the foreground, the gravestone reads 'Unknown German Soldier'.

An ornate grave for a soldier in 9th Company in Infantry Regiment 115, *Schützen* Emil Dessloch, killed on 19 September 1941. Dedication: *Du lebst in uns* (You live in us).

The often-photographed cemetery at Km 41 west of Tobruk on the Via Balbia, where many of the dead from the fighting around Tobruk in April and May 1941 were buried.

THE ENEMY

After every battle there were prisoners who had been captured or rounded up, having been left behind by their own side. These PoWs were usually held back out of sight of the front line. Somewhere out on the flat desert both sides collected their prisoners and put them under guard until they could be transported to an established PoW camp. Whenever a chance presented itself to get a closer look at the living enemy, it was usually taken by any soldiers in the vicinity of the collection points, and the cameras would come out to record the faces of the foe.

They were the English, Scots and Welsh (collectively known to the Germans as 'Tommies' or *Engländer,* 'the English'), and Indians, Irish, Australians, South Africans, New Zealanders, Rhodesians, Greeks, Free French, Poles, Nepalese Ghurkas, Palestinian Jews, Americans, Colonial (African) French, enemies all.

Australians of the 9th Division, taken in 1941.

CHAPTER 25

Indians captured in the advance to El Alamein, June 1942.

Prisoners taken south of Tobruk, early December 1941, waiting for a truck to take them and a guard detail away from the battlefield.

A PoW camp (Italian), somewhere well to the rear of the front in 1941.

An officer sits in the sand under an armed guard at El Alamein in July 1942, while another helmeted 'Tommy' stands looking on.

Interrogation was a reliable and tried source for information on the enemy, here being carried out by an English-speaking officer in June 1942, during fighting for the Gazala Line.

A close look at an enemy oven in a captured camp.

A Wellington bomber that came down behind German lines in the autumn of 1941.

The smiling faces of two Italians photographed by a member of 15th Panzer Division, near Sollum in the summer of 1941.

An interesting discussion on the wharfside in Tripoli in 1941 between a German soldier and two Italians. (The original German caption to this photograph describes it as 'a dud 33 cm naval shell'.)

A small Italian 'tankette', equipped with machine guns and flame throwers, but terribly inadequate for battle with modern anti-tank weapons.

THE ITALIANS

Though Germans and Italians were organised under the same Axis allied command, and fought under one battlefield leader (Rommel) against a common enemy, there was little actual physical contact between the two armies. This was so whether on the battlefield or off it, due mainly to their different training, and the logistical and equipment incompatibilities between the two armies. Language difficulties made most close battlefield cooperation a problem though staff officers were able to co-operate through interpreters. A large number of German speaking 'Italians' from the former Austrian province of the South Tirol served in the German army in Africa as interpreters.

There was some level of social contact in the rear army command areas between those Germans performing administrative duties and their Italian neighbours, both military and civilian. Only those German soldiers stationed in Tripoli for any time had opportunities for close contant with Italian women, and even then it was mainly with those working women who staffed the *Wehrmacht* brothel. (Very few German soldiers serving in combat units ever had such an opportunity.)

German soldiers sympathised with the ordinary Italian soldiers who had to endure an archaic social system entrenched inside the Italian army that allowed a majority of officers to take for themselves the best food and drink, thus enjoying a much higher level of overall creature comfort at the expense of the rank and file soldier.

The Italian army, maligned for so long during and after the war in reporting of the North African war written up in Allied countries, in fact fought bravely on the whole in North Africa. They did this in spite of their antiquated weapons and poor leadership. Indeed, given their poor weaponry and equipment, and deficiencies of leadership, many units of the Italian army showed as much if not more courage on the battlefield than their German allies or their British and Allied enemies.

A road making crew [ta]king stones to build a [p]art of the 'Axis Road' that detoured around Tobruk in 1941, an [a]chievement the Italian [en]gineer battalions were rightly proud of.

A symbolic shot, two Germans and an Italian on a North African beach with their backs to the sea.

A 1943 version of the German *Afrikaner,* with a new uniform made from a generally inferior grade of cloth, a tunic with no pleats on the pockets, and field cap without coloured braid stitched over the cockade. (Charles Hinz)

The giant six-engined air transport Messerschmitt Me323s (*Gigant*) carried their heavy loads of petrol and ammunition across the Mediterranean until the Allied air forces began operations around Sicily. Then German losses were crippling and the few Me323s not shot down were withdrawn from service.

Luftwaffe Flak gunners with an Italian comrade.

THE END, TUNISIA 1943

I n early November 1942 a large American and British army invaded north west Africa, landing along the Atlantic coast of Morocco and on the central Algerian coast in the western Mediterranean. The immediate German response was to rush by air across the Mediterranean a scratch force just strong enough to hold on to a bridgehead in Tunisia, until stronger reinforcements could be moved over by sea. By the time the newly arrived German and Italian armies had joined up with the remnants of Rommel's army inside Tunisia in late 1942, the end phase of the North African campaign was in progress. In the six months of the Tunisian campaign, 147,000 German soldiers (including those forces withdrawn by Rommel from Egypt and Libya) were committed to battle in this Tunisian bridgehead, as the much stronger American and British armies inexorably closed in. The Axis armies were literally fighting with their backs to the sea.

Though the first photo in this section was probably taken at an earlier time, it illustrates the ultimate fate of the Italian-German armies in North Africa, pushed back almost to the sea until they could retreat no further.

The appearance of the German soldier in Tunisia was somewhat different to how he had looked in Libya and Egypt. Apart from the one spectacular parade through Tunis by the Paratroops of *Fallschirmregiment* 5 in mid-November 1942, there were no parades of newly-arrived soldiers in their pith helmets marching down the boulevards of Tunis. The soldiers recently arrived in Tunisia from Europe in their new khaki uniforms went straight to the front. For Rommel's *Afrikakorps* in 1943, after their long retreat from Egypt, uniforms were often patched and worn, and extremely faded. The small amount of spare uniform items in stores carried across with the 5th Panzer Army before the Allies closed the shipping lanes was soon exhausted in early 1943. After satisfying the most urgent needs of the *Afrikakorps*, who had lost their own stores in Egypt and Libya, there was little left over. After this issue of available replacement uniforms, photos taken in 1943 showed combinations of the new darker and older bleached colours, and there was a mixture too of styles with a new model tropical tunic, first used in late 1942, without pleats on the pockets. The German army in Tunisia did not wear the woollen Continental uniform and all German troops sent into action in the Tunisian theatre were issued with standard tropical uniforms.

In the last months of the campaign in Tunisia, nearly all supply space on aircraft and ships arriving across the Mediterranean was used to carry all-important fuel and ammunition, as had been the case at Alamein. New uniforms had a low priority when military tailors could mend old uniforms to prolong their useful life. Bits and pieces of Allied uniforms were also used by German troops in Tunisia, more so than at any other time in North Africa. In Tunisia items of US Army uniform were mixed in with parts of British and Italian uniform, even in a few instances including non-German tunics — something which had not been done before. Only the distinctive German peaked cloth field caps and the German steel helmets remained as the essential parts of German army uniform in Tunisia.

Fewer personal photos survive from the period of the campaign in Tunisia. Not as many personal photos were taken in this period, and of those only a few made it back to Germany. For ordinary soldiers film was almost impossible to acquire in these last months, and in the confusion and destruction of material associated with surrender, many of these personal photos were lost, disappearing in the turmoil of capture.

As the end for the German army in North Africa neared in April and May 1943, morale stayed high right to the end. Even when defeat seemed inevitable, thoughts turned to evacuation to Sicily and to fighting another day in continental Europe, not to surrendering in Africa. This desire to get back to Europe before the approaching end arrived was not just faith in Germany's ability to somehow survive the war successfully; it also meant leave spent at home with family and friends. With the sea lanes closed by Allied air and naval superiority, and the Axis air corridor held open only at great cost to move a few essential supplies, there was no hope in 1943 of any large-scale German and Italian evacuation.

Photos taken in Tunisia do show that there was active support given to the Axis armies by the local Arab population, something that had not happened in Libya or Egypt. In photos of camp scenes taken in 1943 it was common to see Arabs living in close proximity to German troops, with some working as labourers, shifting and storing ammunition, and others carrying out various servant-type duties, behaving exactly like camp followers have done down the centuries in the train of a friendly foreign army. In this case it was more because the nationalistic Arabs in Tunisia saw the Germans as allies against their French colonial masters.

Many vehicles in the German divisions at this time looked as if they had reached the absolute end of their useful lives, after thousands of miles of hard driving across the desert. For the first time large numbers of US Army vehicles became a part of German army camp scenes.

The damage wreaked on a German supply train in central Tunisia in early 194█ The Allied air forces had control of the air by Februa█ 1943.

At the end, the two Axis armies became compressed in the north-eastern part of Tunisia. When over 120,000 German soldiers surrendered between 10 and 13 May 1943, more than half of these troops belonged not to combat units but were part of the various rear echelon support services. (This higher proportion of non-combatant troops in the total number surrendering showed to what extent the front line units had been losing their fighting strength.) For the rear area units, pushed back behind the shrinking front with no heavy weapons or ammunition, organised resistance was impossible, even had they been equipped to perform it. After the last surrenders on 13 May, all German troops were held at first in PoW 'cages', large tracts of flat ground laid out with German tents enclosed by perimeter fences of barbed wire and Allied guards. Later the German PoWs were transferred to proper PoW camps in Algeria or Egypt before being shipped off to other camps in the USA, Canada or the United Kingdom.

Inside the PoW cages the spirit of the *Afrikakorps* lived on, and the old familiar military discipline that had held them together in the field asserted itself in organising self-help in the camps. The welfare of all PoWs had to be entrusted to the tried and trusted systems of German military organisation. This was especially so in the case of personal hygiene and sanitary arrangements, food preparation and its distribution, and getting medical care to those who needed it.

After the surrender of the Axis military command in Tunisia in May 1943, the only German military presence in North Africa was the occasional flight by high altitude reconnaissance Messerschmitt Bf110s based at Foggia in southern Italy. These specially lightened aircraft with their high resolution cameras used forward airfields in Crete and Sicily or Sardinia for refuelling stops. They flew from the end of 1942 until the autumn of 1943, their flights covering the long coastline from the Nile delta to Algiers.

A very different terrain was encountered the further north one went in Tunisia. Shown here is a typical valley scene in central Tunisia, with an Arab village nestled against the side of a hill high above a wadi. (Dieter Hellriegel)

Dieter Hellriegel (right) and Unteroffizier Müller, in front of the Company HQ tent of the 2nd (Panzer) Company of Rommel's Kamptstaffel, near Sfax in March 1943. (Dieter Hellriegel)

Snap taken by an American GI of four German PoWs in captivity after the general surrender of 12/13 May 1943.

'FOR THE RECORD'

LIBYA, NOVEMBER-DECEMBER 1941

T he following photos were taken by members of the motorised company of military war correspondents (*Kriegsberichter*) attached to the *Afrikakorps* and commanded by Sonderführer Zwilling. They were taken between mid-November 1941 and late December 1941 and show scenes on and off battlefields that stretched from the Egyptian border at Sollum and Capuzzo to Tobruk and the many points in between, and back to the area near El Agheila on the Gulf of Sirte. This time marks the period of the North African campaign known to the Germans as the Winter Battle.

The few photos shown here represent a small part of the some 10,000 (270 x 36 frame 35mm spools) taken by this one company in a month and a half of extremely heavy fighting. They are representative of those specially noted as being intended for official military archive files, stamped on the back, *Nur für den Dienstgebrauch* (FOR SERVICE USE ONLY). Many of the remaining photos taken would have been sent back to Germany as illustrations for newspaper and magazine stories.

The following photos would have ended up in an official military archive, mounted on a cardboard-backed A4 size page under the headings *Heeresfilmstelle* and *Bildarchiv*. These standard *Wehrmacht* archive cards recorded a description of the scene depicted in the photo, along with information as to its time and place and identifying the unit concerned.

The special significance of these particular photos is that they show that face of the *Afrikakorps,* and its battlefields, that the Germany army considered making its own official record.

November 1941, the opening of the Winter Battle brought early successes – while this 88 mm gun moves up towards the front.

CHAPTER 28

What next? Snapped on the afternoon of 23 November, the day of the famous 'Sunday Battle', a PzIII from 15 Pz.Div. and a staff car showing the commander's pennant of a motorised infantry battalion wait for orders.

PoWs from the 4th Indian Division, captured early [in] the fighting, Sikhs who have evidently lost their turbans.

Radio transciever of a regimental HQ on the *Sollumfront*, with signaller encoding a message (the man at rear holds a morse key device).

Italians with a Molotov Cocktail made from a champagne bottle with a flare pistol cartridge and fuse attached.

Batches of prisoners rounded up in the desert, here held under the gaze of two guards with MG34 machine gun. The 'Ib' daubed on the side of the vehicle is interesting, identifying it as belonging to a staff officer (logistics) attached to a divisional rear echelon column.

The scene on 24 November, south-west of Halfaya, the wreckage from the NZ 5th Brigade positions over-run by Pz.Rgt.5.

24 November 1941, near Sidi Omar, the body of a dead British soldier lying behind a small parapet of rocks, killed by airburst artillery shrapnel.

173

Photographed on 25 November, on the Sollumfront, two shots of a knocked out British Matilda Infantry Tank with the name 'Park Royal'. In the second shot, two Germans are pulling the limp body of a crewman through the hatch in the turret roof. The dead crewman's hair is matted with blood, indicating he may have received a fatal head wound. A British tank man (in beret) stands by watching.

1 December 1941, a PzIV moves past the photographer's camera lens near Bardia.

Another British tank crewman, probably from the same tank (this photo is four frames on from the previous shot on the very same spool) receives an abdominal injection of morphine from a helmeted German soldier. The British soldier, obviously in great pain, has worked up a mound of sand under his right boot as he convulsively bends and straightens his leg.

To increase the volume of supplies that could be flown in across the Mediterranean, the Ju 52s and bombers such as the He 111 and the Ju 88 were used to tow gliders which were loaded up with much-needed supplies. These four photos show one such glider, a Gotha 242, being unloaded at El Adem and then taking off again behind a Ju 52 heading for Crete to collect another cargo.

During the German withdrawal to the west on
5 December, this very typical view was taken of a small
group of German infantry in a shallow wadi, doing the
things all soldiers do during a pause in a battle – just
sitting and looking around, cleaning weapons that have
recently been fired, eating a quick snack, unloading and
repacking the military and personal gear every soldier
carried around with him, and all around are the bundles
of field gear put down on the ground until the order to
move again is given by the officers and NCOs.

Official shot of the official photographer, Sonderführer Zwilling,
with his Leica and two Agfa cameras, snapped by one of his
men south-west of Tobruk on 5 December 1941. On this day,
Rommel ordered the DAK to pull back from around Tobruk. In
the background, an 88mm gun and its crew packed up for
travel drive past heading for new positions further to the west.

By 6th December, the Afrikakorps was digging in near
Gazala in its withdrawl to the west, and this 5 cm
PAK38 anti-tank gun and its crew make a familiar
combination of shapes – a low parapet of rocks, gun
and crew with their individual weapons and gear close
at hand. It was common practice if the ground could be
broken to dig a trench inside the rock wall. (In the
Libyan desert today these low horseshoe shaped
mounds of rocks still survive, showing where the anti-
tank gunners once took up their positions.)

Sitzkrieg, the 'Sitdown War'. By late December 1941 the
Afrikakorps were back in old positions of nine months ago in
front of El Agheila, and the Winter Battle was over.

ERNST ZWILLING

O f the many thousands of photos taken by Germans during the North African campaign of World War II, one photographer took more than any other individual. This man was Ernst Zwilling, a *Luftwaffe Sonderführer,* who headed the company of official photographers sent to Libya in early March 1941 to record the German *Wehrmacht* in the North African desert. For the next two years he took tens of thousands of photos of the North African battlefields, seen from the German side. As the top ranking official photographer, he had constant and easy access to Rommel and his staff, and to the other main unit commanders too. Very many of the well-known shots of the German army and its commanders in North Africa are by Zwilling.

Ernst Zwilling's photos have been used as illustrations by nearly every author who has written on the subject of the *Afrikakorps* since World War II. His photos are to be found today in large numbers in military and state photo archives in the United States, England, Germany and France, where the largest number of his photos are held in Paris by EPCA, the French army's photo library. However, none of these photos acknowledge Ernst Zwilling by name as the photographer, and whenever they are reproduced the photos show the archive as the source, and the owner, of the photo.

Rommel in late 1941, with his *Ia Oberstleutnant* Westphal at right in dark glasses, and chief of staff General Gause with back to camera.

CHAPTER 29

This remarkable man was born on 25 September 1904 in the small Austrian town of Esseg. His family were well off and had provided generations of officers for the Austrian army. The young Ernst Zwilling developed a passion for hunting wild game, travelling frequently to the former German colony of the Cameroons to indulge himself in this rich man's sport. (After 1919 *Kamerun,* as it had been known, was ruled by France under a League of Nations mandate.) Ernst Zwilling was well known before 1939 as the white hunter who went further and for longer into the bush than other hunters. It was here he became as expert with a camera as he was with a rifle. He was educated as a geographer and while on his hunting safaris he also worked on mapping and recording the habitat of west African wildlife.

With this background it was not surprising that Ernst Zwilling was selected in early 1941 to head the small detachment of photographers being sent to Libya with General Rommel's *Afrikakorps.* Zwilling was given the rank of *Sonderführer,* a specialist with officer rank status. The unit he commanded was *Luftwaffe Kriegsberichter Kompanie 7 (mot)* or the 7th Company (motorised) of Air Force War Correspondents. While attached to the *Luftwaffe,* this unit was in fact deployed in North Africa to record all aspects of the German military presence there. Indeed, by far the greater part of Zwilling's own work was concerned with the German army and its commanders, and not the *Luftwaffe.* There were, of course, many other German military photographers in Africa, some in Zwilling's own unit, and there were more who came and went on special secondment. But it was Zwilling himself who took most of the now well-known shots of Rommel and other famous commanders who served with Rommel in Africa.

Zwilling was decorated for his bravery while he was in North Africa, in circumstances most war correspondents were not likely to find themselves in. While taking photos of an 88-mm gun crew of *I Abteilung Flak Regiment 33* in June 1941 on the Egyptian border, the gun received a near hit that killed and wounded most of the gun crew. The gun itself was not put out of action and Zwilling dropped his camera to take his place with the surviving crew as one of the loaders handling the 88-mm shells. For this action, which drove off a strong British tank force, inflicting heavy losses on the British, Zwilling was later awarded the Iron Cross 2nd Class.

After the surrender of the German and Italian armies in May 1943 in Africa, Zwilling continued his work as a photographer and war correspondent, serving in the Italian theatre and in the Balkans. He also spent some of this time on Crete and the Greek islands of the Aegean Sea. At the end of the war he was captured by the Red Army and spent two years in captivity as a PoW in the Soviet Union.

By 1950 Zwilling was able to return to Africa, both as a hunter and a photographer. He made many journeys to his old hunting grounds in French Equatorial Africa and organised three expeditions to Lake Chad. He also made journeys through the Sahara, and led expeditions into central Africa, up the Congo studying the pygmies and exploring the hinterland of Angola. In the 1970s the now Professor Zwilling was dividing his time between an academic life lecturing in Europe and running a safari business for 'white hunters' operating in Uganda and Kenya. By this time Ernst Zwilling had become a committed conservationist and he urged his clients to use a camera instead of a bullet to shoot their prey.

In November 1990 Ernst Zwilling died, in Vienna, in his eighty-seventh year. In his life he had been a hunter, an explorer, an author, and had mapped many unmapped parts of central and west Africa, photographed the highest and lowest ranking members of the German army at war for four years in Africa and southern Europe, spent two years in a Soviet PoW camp, had reclaimed his scholarly reputation as an African 'expert' after the war and was rewarded with academic honours, had built up a successful safari business for hunters of big game in east Africa, and ended his life as a prominent supporter of international conservation movements based in Africa.

The photos reproduced here were obtained from Ernst Zwilling by Charles Hinz, a long time acquaintance of Zwilling's and himself an authority on the German *Afrikakorps*. These few photographs are only a token representation of Ernst Zwilling's work with a camera, but at last his name can be shown here in print in company with his photos.

...mel, in a 1942 ...ile shot, with *Oberst* ...in Wolz, commander ...*uftwaffe* Flak ...iment 135.

Rommel in conference with Italian and German unit commanders.

Rommel in a typical pose, wearing his distinctive olive-coloured leather greatcoat, tartan scarf, and the British anti-gas goggles on his cap, that marks this photo as one taken in the winter of 1941/42.

A view of *Hauptmann* Walter Fromm, the Commander of I/Flak Rgt.33, Knight's Cross winner and veteran of the Spanish Civil War.

The *Luftwaffe Feldmarschall* Albert Kesselring, German commander of the Mediterranean theatre and Rommel immediate superior, taken in the early summer of 194

Feldwebel Reinhard Melzer, another of the 88mm gunners of I/Flak Reg.33, who won his Knight's Cross in the fighting of June 1941, here examining the entry hole of an 88mm round in a British Matilda tank.

ERNST ZWILLING

Luftwaffe Medical Surgeon-General
Generaloberststabsarzt Dr Hippke
visited Africa in the late 1941.
(Walter Fromm at left of this photo.)

End of day, vehicles are formed into a
close ring for the night and the sentries
are posted. This practice was followed
for much of the fighting in November-
December 1941 over the open desert
of eastern Cyrenaica.

The moment of firing by a well dug-in
88mm. Notice the cloud of dust raised
from the muzzle blast.

181

Artillery gunner checks the optical sight on a 10.5 cm field howitzer.

Picking over a captured British food dump. (Note the smoke on the horizon, indicating burning vehicles.)

Regimental HQ signals vehicles.

88mm gun crew, during a lull in action during the Winter Battle of November-December 1941.

...e Commander of the DAK in early 1942, General Ludwig Crüwell (centre). ...e German officer at left is Major Max Hecht, a ...gimental Flak commander and later Knight's Cross holder.

The inevitable sequel to battle, fatigue-induced sleep.

THE FORGOTTEN AFRICAN
(*DER VERGESSENE AFRIKANER*)

O ne of the most enduring and widely held images the soldiers of the *Afrikakorps* had of themselves was as a forsaken and largely forgotten part of the German *Wehrmacht*.

From very early on in the campaign it was evident to even the lowest ranking German soldier that the Axis position in North Africa was an uncertain one with tenuous supply lines running across the Mediterranean under attack by British naval and air forces. Many had personally experienced just such a terrifying attack during their own crossing to Africa.

Every German soldier knew of mail posted from home that had simply not arrived, a sure sign that ships and aircraft carrying mail were not reaching Africa. Everyone experienced the almost constant shortages of food, of uniforms and basic field equipment, of vehicles and spare parts, of weapons, and indeed of everything a modern army needed to fight with. It was common knowledge that Rommel gave priority to supplies of ammunition and petrol, yet even these two essential elements of modern warfare were often in short supply too. Their high morale, a boundless confidence in Rommel's leadership, trust in their weapons and training — all of these things in the end were not enough by themselves for the *Afrikakorps* to win every battle when the means of fighting had to be so carefully rationed.

The *Afrikakorps* soldiers handled this grim situation in the way soldiers react to such news, with the peculiar brand of black humour that stated the worst possible future scenario through ironic narrative story and graffiti. There were many variations to the theme that after the end of the war the survivors of the *Afrikakorps* would become a new 'African'* tribe, forlornly wandering the desert dressed in ragged remnants of military uniform and bits of Arab dress, waiting in vain for repatriation to Germany. In many of these stories 1945 was picked as the end of the war, an uncanny prediction.

The drawing shown [right] was photographed in late 1941 by a South African soldier on the walls of the Sollum barracks. This graphic sketch by an anonymous German expresses so well the feelings of many *Afrikakorps* soldiers, of being abandoned in desolate conditions, starved of supplies by their parent army organisation, and thus becoming 'forgotten Africans'.

* The *Afrikakorps* soldiers' slang term for themselves was 'Afrikaner', literally 'African' (i.e. 'a native inhabitant of the African continent'.)   *Jan Wessels*

184